MOM SPELLED BACKWARDS IS TIRED

mom
spelled
backwards
is tired

mom spelled backwards is tired ANN RUDY

THE BOBBS-MERRILL COMPANY, INC.
INDIANAPOLIS · NEW YORK

Library of Congress Cataloging in Publication Data

Rudy, Ann.
　Mom spelled backwards is tired.

　　1. Family–United States–Anecdotes, facetiae,
satire, etc.   I. Title.
HQ536.R84　　301.42′02′07　　　79-55442
ISBN 0-672-52627-1

Designed by Jean Callan King
Manufactured in the United States of America

First printing

To my children, Robin and Andrew,
and my husband, Ralph

With a special salute to every woman
who has ever left a warm bed at 2 A.M.
in response to her child's call:
"Mom, come quick! I think I'm gonna
throw up,"
and arrived . . . too late

Contents ❦

Introduction 🦋 When Norman Mailer

said, "Face it, girls, you have a womb" (it's okay, Norman, you can say uterus), he wasn't telling us anything. Speaking for myself, I can say that my womb–to use that charming medieval terminology–has come in pretty handy. I have used it as nature intended, and I wonder if Norman can say as much about his liver.

The issue of said womb has qualified me for membership in that great legion of women called moms. And regardless of what Philip Wylie had to say about us, we are generally a pretty decent lot. Because even if Philip had been my son, he could have counted on me to whack him between the shoulder blades had he choked on a button. And hard, too.

But motherhood involves more than keeping breath and broth in tiny mouths that may someday grow up to criticize and ask for money all the time. Soon after a woman is told to bear down in the delivery room, she is required to bear up and up and up. This can be tiring–especially if she has seen too many Ginger Rogers movies and likes to tap-dance.

But it's worth it. Don't ask me why, but every moment is . . . worth it.

MOM SPELLED BACKWARDS IS TIRED

Cementing Family Ties with Oatmeal

🐝 It's Mother of the Year time again, and like a lot of you out there, I didn't win. But do you think that made me snippy at the breakfast table?

Yes. It's not as if it were a drawing; I never expect to win those turkeys and new cars. But when a selection was to be made from all the women in the country, I'll have to admit I had hopes. I mean, it certainly ought to be worth a nomination that I always manage to get up and fix everybody a hot breakfast—even if nobody wants it.

Just yesterday I called "Hot oatmeal!" down the hall and was met with silence. "Hot oatmeal!" I repeated, and one kid shuffled into the kitchen, looked at me dimly, and said, "I hate oatmeal."

But do you think I paid any attention to him? Of course not. I lobbed a lump of oatmeal into a bowl and shoved it at him. "Eat that," I threatened, "or you'll never make it to the eighth grade." That's what I call communication. He not only ate it, he winked at me. Either he winked at me or he had developed a tic in his right eye.

Then my daughter emerged from her room, and I gave her what a psychologist would call supportive love.

"I hate my hair," she exploded as she danced across the kitchen in a vicious little twostep and broke her comb in half.

"Sit down and eat your oatmeal," I said evenly, "or I'll take my credit cards and run away from home, and you'll never see me again."

She sat right down and dug into her oatmeal, and I'm not sure, but I think she winked at me, too.

As I say, I really don't understand why I didn't even get honorable mention.

Heaven knows I'm always talking to my kids, and I have more hot oatmeal on hand than I know what to do with. Enough to fill the biggest Mother of the Year trophy going.

Keeping Up with the Brownings 🐝 Some people may worry

about keeping up with The Joneses, but I worry about keeping up with The Brownings.

How do you suppose Elizabeth ever managed to write such moving love poems as those found in *Sonnets from the Portuguese* while she was sick in bed and Robert was in the kitchen rattling pans? Last week when I was in bed with the flu, all I felt like writing to my husband was a crank note.

I wonder if Robert ever brought Elizabeth a flaming lamb chop on a paper plate for dinner. If he did, I'll bet he didn't give her a spoon to eat it with.

"What's that brown stuff all over your shirt?" I asked my husband as I spooned up the lamb chop.

"It's coffee," he said. "I left the lid off while it was perking."

Okay, so he isn't Betty Crocker. But it's more than just that. There were ominous sounds from the kitchen which any woman, no matter how sick, would rise on one elbow about. Like a bottle cap being gnawed up by the garbage disposer. Or shattering glass followed by low mutterings. And that unidentified thud which could have been anything from the collapse of a tired husband to the capsizing of the refrigerator.

"Are you all right, dear?" I called out weakly in my best Victorian voice; and he hollered back, "Hell, no, I'm not all right. The ironing board just jumped out at me from the broom closet. I think my nose is fractured." Somehow, verbal exchanges like that cancel out the ro-

2

mantic poem inspiration. But they certainly make you
want to get well.

I picked up a pencil and paper, thought for a minute,
and jotted, "When will you be out of my kitchen? Let me
count the days."

The Brownings may not have put it quite that way, but
that's about as fired up as a girl can get on one burned
lamp chop.

Love Once Easy
To Pocket 🐛 During my sixth-grade career there

was a little boy named Johnny who used to slip love
notes into the pocket of my red sweater as it hung in the
cloakroom during recess. My mother wondered why I had
so many colds, and I can tell her now what I couldn't tell
her then: I never, ever wore that sweater during recess or
Johnny wouldn't have had a chance to secrete those
marvelous little missives.

I hadn't thought of him in years, but I did the other
day. I bought a sweater, and when I put my hand into
the pocket I felt a small slip of paper.

Suddenly I was eleven again. I slowly extracted the note
and opened it with racing heart. "Inspected by No. 6," it
read, and suddenly I was forty again. I suppose if the
sweater had been missing a button, No. 6 would have
caught it from whoever lowers the boom on negligent
inspectors. And I guess that's as it should be, but I can't
help wondering if the sweater company isn't missing an
opportunity.

"Inspected by No. 6" is today all the way–and part of
the reason people take to the seashore and mountains in
search of something real. It probably wouldn't cost much
more to put a bigger piece of paper into sweater pockets.

A paper big enough to carry a message with warmth. Something like, "You are the prettiest girl in the whole world. It doesn't matter to me that you were the first one down in the spelling bee. Your loving inspector, No. 6."

I'll tell you one thing: that company would get a lot fewer complaints. I wouldn't care if all the buttons were missing, if only No. 6 had heart.

Johnny had the secret. He let me know how much he cared, and I let him copy all my arithmetic. And when my answers were wrong, he still didn't give up–he copied my geography maps. That's class with a capital K.

Personally, sweater makers of America, I'd rather not have my sweater inspected if it's going to lead to heartbreak. Either say you love me or shut up.

The Short, Happy Life of Mother Macomber 🐘 When I was about

seven, I saw a movie which starred Sabu, the Indian elephant boy. In it, elephants, when they sickened, lumbered through the dense jungle to a mysterious far-off place where they apparently fell over and died.

Sabu was always looking for the elephant graveyard–tiptoeing along behind ailing elephants in hopes of finding their vast final resting place and the treasure of ivory that lay waiting. The elephants and the treasure always eluded him.

I feel a lot like Sabu. Only what I'm tiptoeing after isn't an elephant, but my kids. And I'm not looking for ivory but for that elusive missing sock or lost sweater or, believe it or not, their underwear. I'm convinced that all their stuff I can't find is in the elephant graveyard.

I have seventeen socks with no mates in my laundry basket. And it turns out I'm no matchmaker. Holding one of the new single socks, I approached my son with what I hoped was an air of authority. "Listen here," I said, "your father laid out two dollars for this pair of socks, and you've already lost one. Where is it?"

He looked innocently at the dangling sock and said, "I dunno."

And he doesn't. Just like he doesn't know where his new underwear is. While looking through his bureau in search of it, I came across a pair of BVDs big enough for Alfred Hitchcock and older than Gabby Hayes. "How many times have I told you," I said, "if you're going to bring home somebody else's underwear, trade up?"

But he doesn't pay any attention to me, any more than my daughter does when I call after her, "Come back with my new sweater–what happened to the one I bought you?"

Someday I'll find those missing socks, the sweater and the underwear. They've got to be out there somewhere. Sabu never gave up, and neither will I.

Kitchen Canards and How To Cook Them 🐝 When I cook, I don't want

anybody in my kitchen.

It's not that I'm such an expert; just that I'm afraid someone will find out what I'm up to. I am a third-generation charlatan.

There are things going on in my kitchen that would curl your bacon. It's a lot worse than my fudge turning to brown cement, and it goes a bit further than my eggnogs not nogging.

I am the only woman I know who can go into a kitchen, do nothing and emerge with a hot meal under way. That's because I'm the only woman I know whose cookbook contains nothing but phone numbers.

But do you have any idea how difficult it is to make one of those delivered dinners look home-cooked? I mean if you have four couples sitting around your living room waiting for you to be Julia Child, what do you do when the doorbell rings and it's a guy with ten paper plates full of chicken? And he is driving a delivery truck with a red light flashing on the hood like a rescue unit?

For openers, you tuck those ten plates under one arm and do a quarterback sneak into the kitchen. Then you pry them open and throw the contents onto waiting plates–plates that contain decoys.

A delivered-dinner decoy is something that makes your guests ask, "Did she, or didn't she?" Homemade rolls out of frozen tubes, radishes cut like roses by your little boy with his Scout knife, and a blob of marmalade made by an anonymous member of your church guild. And don't forget the parsley. (If you can count on nobody eating it, use plastic.)

As for dessert, nobody delivers that, so you will have to count on your dinner wine. Just keep filling those glasses and smiling, and then put down dessert plates with nothing on them.

A guest with a fifth of wine under his cummerbund will regard an empty dessert plate as his own doing. He may even compliment you on your culinary achievement.

In which case, you simply twist one corner of your apron, lower your eyes and say, "It was nothing." That's what I call telling it like it is.

Sex and the Single Six-Year-Old 🐝 Psychologists say it is best not to bring up the facts of life until your child does. Then,

his questions should be answered matter-of-factly.

That sounds reasonable enough. So I told my husband: "Stop asking him if he has anything on his mind during those fishing trips of yours. And don't lock yourself up in your study with him every six months. When the kid wants to know, he'll ask."

Little did I know he would ask me. And not on a fishing trip or behind closed doors, but on our way into a crowded toy store.

His was the kind of gut-bucket question that would have stunned a gynecologist–asked in a tone I believe musicians refer to as fortissimo. Not only did we have the attention of everybody in the toy store, but three shoe salesmen from next door came in to hear my answer.

I didn't have one right away. Instead, I stalled for time while trying to interest him in a plastic bow and arrow set. "Look here," I said, "you could kill the dog across the street with this."

But he failed to respond, and I knew I would have to come up with something more substantial–and quickly. He had already repeated the question twice, and our audience had now closed in to a tight little circle.

"Well," I began, as matter-of-factly as I could, "that's something you will have to ask your father."

Talk about a cop-out. I not only lost my standing as a psychologist; I lost my audience. Now I know how an author feels when his play closes after two nights.

The shoe salesmen shuffled out, and if they had paid admission they would have asked for their money back. Everybody else returned to buying wooden puzzles or two-inch racing cars.

And my son found himself in the usual middle-class dilemma: he couldn't find anything in the toy store he didn't already have. Except the answer to his question. Maybe we could give it to him for Christmas.

The Gift of Gas 🦋 Pretty soon it won't be

unreasonable to say, "Promise her anything, but give her
gasoline."

So far, I haven't had to line up to fill my tank, but as
the price of gas continues to rise, and it becomes in
shorter and shorter supply, its very scarcity and expense
will move it from the "fill 'er up" vernacular to "A whole
gallon for me? You shouldn't have!"

At Christmas, business firms will stop handing out free
liquor to their clients and give them instead a couple of
gallons of high octane all done up in red cellophane.

Of course there will be some clients who will drink it
anyway; simply because it is always difficult to teach an
old drunk new tricks, but it will help them cut down on
their smoking.

A wife, stuck for what to give her mother-in-law for her
birthday, can present ten gallons and a road map. Five
gallons, even. OK, a quart–if it will get her off the sofa
and down the driveway.

But I hope nobody gives me gas as a present, because I
think I may take to my bike and stop driving completely.
I want to be the first woman on my block to park her car
in the living room as an art object. Then when the kids
call from two blocks away and want me to drive them
home, I'll say, "You know I've planted fern in our
backseat. Walk."

And if they don't like it, I'll promise them a couple of
gallons in yellow gift wrap the day they get their driver's
license–so when they want to run away from home, I will
have done my part toward making their dreams come
true. What's a mother for?

So it may be that we will be thinking of gasoline in an
entirely new framework sooner than we realize. Not
something pumped into our cars by a fellow in baggy
pants with a rag in his back pocket, but a rare wine–*lieb-*

fraumilch from the deep strata of our own mother earth.
Just a drop, please.

The Junk-Mail Connection 🐝 I've

solved the junk-mail problem at our house by renaming
the dog. Our big black Newfoundland, formerly known as
Noche after the night of the same color, is now
"Occupant."

I stumbled across the idea quite by accident one day
while reading through a pile of occupant mail that I
couldn't bear to throw away. Envelopes marked "Open
immediately. Valuable coupon inside" proved, time and
again, to be not only worthless but downright insulting.

I keep getting hints from deodorant soap companies and
little innuendos from book sellers which imply that I'd
better update my reading or I'll be a social failure.
Frankly, I don't know of a sweeter-smelling housewife
than myself, and when it comes to being informed, I
know the exact date that Halley's comet didn't hit.

So who needs junk mail?

Certainly not I, so I took to tossing it aside with
complete abandon—until I noticed one day that Noche fell
upon it eagerly and chewed it happily to bits.

It had the delicious aroma of mailman on it. So I took
the mailman aside and said, "Look, you've been putting a
lot of stuff addressed to the dog in my mailbox.
'Occupant' over there doesn't like that." The mailman
looked at the dog, who was snarling as usual, and
promised it wouldn't happen again.

"Well, I hope not," I said. "Just toss him his mail after
this and 'Occupant' will leave you alone."

Now everybody's happy. The mailman feels safer, the
dog's teeth are cleaner, and I am free to read the really

important stuff. Like bills, tax notices, and letters from my mother-in-law.

Now if I can just keep "Occupant" from sending away for all those books, I'll have it made.

Teacher, You're My Pet 🍎 When it

comes to favorite teachers, I'll have to admit I never had one. I was the kind of kid who wasn't teacher's pet–or pest. I was just there. Mostly, I waited for the bell to ring and tried to think up ways to remember my times tables without learning them. It seemed as though neither one would ever happen.

But now that my boy is a sixth grader, I do have a favorite teacher. She is not his teacher in particular, but that great faceless sixth-grade teacher everywhere.

Whatever her name, she is my favorite. Because a mother can't help admiring a woman who spends six hours a day, five days a week, with thirty-two eleven-year-olds and is still smiling–or trying to–at the end of the year. I'd throw her a bouquet if she were still standing.

Just yesterday I asked my son, after he'd been absent for a week with flu, if he was able to pick up right where he'd left off at school.

"Oh, yes," he replied happily. "I just shot a few rubber bands and threw a couple spitballs, and everything was back to normal." I've had other glimpses of what goes on in the sixth grade, but I'd rather not think about them now.

It is enough to remember the night he had eight classmates over for a dinner-slumber party. I thought they were exchange students. None of them understood English.

"Time to quit punching each other," I said gaily as the dinner hour approached. "The first one to stop bleeding gets an extra hamburger."

They paid no attention. I almost called Hot Line for help, but I wasn't sure they handled that sort of thing.

And to think his teacher manages to get facts into their heads. And gets them to produce a handmade Mother's Day card.

If I didn't know it was happening, I wouldn't believe it. She is truly cool, that sixth-grade teacher, and I can only hope she realizes that mothers everywhere salute her.

Signs of the Times 🐝 I have seen the
ultimate in bumper sticker philosophy.

As I sat entombed in my car, helpless in a lane of clotted late-afternoon traffic, two words on the bumper ahead of me caught my eye. "Feel Good," they instructed.

I don't mean to say I don't think there was somebody somewhere feeling good. Probably the man who collected 49 cents for that bumper sticker was at home on his patio feeling good.

It's just that slogans for instant adjustment seem such a waste of good bumper space.

The fellow who cut in front of me the other day–from the right lane doing 70–had a message for me as he sped off into oblivion: "Be Nice," his bumper said.

I'll try, mister, I'll try. But you'll have to realize that as soon as you passed me I choked up. It wasn't your message that did it either; your muffler was leaking. Be nice yourself.

And how about that "Smile" command? You are driving along toward the dentist's office with a toothache and you see that magic word in hot pink on the rear window in front of you. So you smile like Humphrey Bogart, and nothing changes except the traffic light–turning green so you will be on time for the novocain.

I have no signs of anything but wear and tear on my bumper and probably never will have. It's not that I have nothing to say to the guy in back of me; it's just that if I'm going to tell him how to feel or what to do, I'd rather have him look me in the eye instead of the back of my neck.

And the next time I see somebody with a "Have you hugged your kid today?" sticker on display, I certainly hope he will pull over and let me pass him so I can get home and go to work on it.

My Money or Yours? 🐝 How much allowance you give your child may vary, but the decision to put him on the dole usually takes place in the five-and-ten.

The young child discovers the joys of the dime store at an early age, and at first it seems like a harmless enough indulgence. A balloon keeps him–and you–happy all the way home and for three hours thereafter.

Then the balloon pops, and there is a small crisis during which you promise him a return trip to the five-and-ten for something even nicer. Thus begins a gradual escalation of nickel-and-dime treats until, by the time the kid is tall enough to see over the edge of the counter, he has gone through the entire stock of cheap thrills.

He has had measles and everything else under 39 cents twice. Then one day, shortly after he has learned to read, he discovers that the big stuff is kept on the shelf above the counter.

"Hey, mom," he exclaims, "look! A 500-piece erector set!"

"Yes," you answer, moving away, "I saw it. How'd you like another bag of plastic soldiers?"

"Naw, I'm sick of those. I want that," he replies, and takes his stand firmly in the middle of the main aisle.

Besides the $19.95 price tag–which seems a little incongruous for the five-and-ten–there is a can of spray paint connected with that erector set. Red spray enamel in the hands of a seven-year-old? It's a mother's nightmare.

You grasp his upper arm the way you did the day he put the cat in the dryer. "Look, that's $20. You have to save for something like that."

He looks at you blankly and asks, "Save? What's that?" Hurriedly you whisper the secrets of Wall Street and high finance into his small ear; you climax these revelations with the promise of his very own allowance of 25 cents a week. "You mean my own money to do whatever I want with?" he asks.

"Exactly," you answer, handing over the quarter.

He is so thrilled you wonder why you didn't think of it three thousand crayons ago. Not only does he forget about the erector set; it cuts down on your time in the five-and-ten as well.

"What a rook," he observes, scanning the merchandise. "I'm gonna save my dough."

Cats Have No Masters–
Only Ph.D.s 🦋 The cat lover, I have noticed, is

usually an intellectual. That probably explains why I can't stand cats.

I've tried; I really have. I went so far as to present my daughter with one, even though my mother told me cats sometimes suck your breath. "Here," I said to my child, "is the cat you always wanted. Look out it doesn't suck your breath."

Now isn't that fair enough? We named him Sam and he did not suck her breath. Far from it. Sam jumped out our kitchen window two days after we took him in and became the neighborhood rake. He came home only to eat–delicately–his canned fish.

Then one day he came home and sat gracefully by the Boston fern and eyed me all afternoon. This is it, I thought; now he is going to suck my breath.

But I was wrong. That night Sam entered the linen closet at 11:05 and delivered six scrawny kittens.

And that's why I can't stand cats. They never tell you anything. They are composed, secretive, aloof and absolutely enigmatic. You can't catch a cat's eye and say, "Come here, boy," like you do to a dog, and have that cat scamper over and lick your hand. Oh, no. The cat will look at you, think about it, and lick his own paw. It's infuriating–that sort of independence.

Have you ever seen a cat sit up and beg? Or jump up and down and whine at the sound of car keys jingling? Give me a dog any old time. A cat never wags his tail except just before he pounces on something smaller than himself. And even then he only wags the tip.

Sam must have known, in her heart, how I felt about cats. Because one day she simply gave me one long, last gaze and walked out. I think she's doing graduate work at UCLA.

Two Dogs Don't Make a Right 🐝 We have decided to get a

second dog–that is, a dog in addition to the one we already have.

But nobody seems to understand. People keep asking,
"What are you going to do with your other dog?"
Strange, nobody asked what we were going to do with
our other kid when I found out I was going to have a
second.

In the first place, the dog we have now hardly qualifies
as a dog. Due to emotional problems, he not only is
effeminate; he is afraid to get out from under the dining
room table. Consequently, to balance things out, we have
decided on a 200-pound Newfoundland. A dog that size
won't be able to get under the dining room table even if
he wants to.

That means he will be willing to run and romp with our
boy, who might hug anything under 170 pounds to death.
Nana, of Peter Pan fame, was a Newfoundland, and you
know what a slick job she did of looking after the
children.

I figure any dog that weighs 90 pounds more than I do
ought to be able to watch kids and help out around the
house. You might think that for what it will cost me to
feed such a dog, I could hire a full-time maid and butler
as well.

But not according to the man who sold me the dog. He
said Newfoundlands have a very low metabolism. That
means they just don't burn as many calories as regular
dogs.

"Lady," the kennel man promised, "you won't have to
give this dog more than twelve cups of kibble a day."
And at first they don't even eat that much.

But after he has been housebroken, sent to obedience
school, given $50 worth of shots and chewed up half my
house—then he begins to eat the twelve cups of kibble a
day.

By that time, of course, he will be washing dishes,
tucking the kids in, and chasing people away from my
front door. It sounds like a fantastic deal to me. Just

think, a live-in dog.

He won't be ready to leave the kennel for another two weeks, at which time his eyes will be open. My husband says the dog's eyes will be open before mine are. What do you suppose he means by that?

Just Call Her Your Husband's Mother for Short 🍎

There's never been much question about what to call your mother-in-law when she isn't around, but what do you call her to her face?

"Mother" has always seemed to me a word reserved for one's own. I mean, I might be crazy over my mother-in-law, but she could never compete with my childhood images of mama at the back door handing out hot buttermilk biscuits to me and my neighborhood pals. And it wasn't *her* hand that held my five-year-old hand so I could sleep after waking to the terrifying sounds of the local fire engine.

If one waits long enough, and mother-in-law stays in her corner long enough, the marriage may be blessed with children, and then the problem is partially solved by rolling out such benign words as Gaga, Nana, and good old grandma. But for the wife, the mother-in-law is still not her grandma.

And forget instructions to call her whatever makes you comfortable. I feel comfortable with first names, but when I tried it, the feeling wasn't mutual. I have a mother-in-law who can smile with one eye and cry with the other, and when I said, "How about another helping of yams, Bertha?" her left eye filled.

So, over the years, I have managed by various methods. "Ask your mother if she would like more yams," is a good one. Or catch her eye and hold up the yams while raising your eyebrows in question. Try pointing and saying "she" (but don't try this one unless you want to see both eyes fill).

Using names, after all, is simply a way of getting a person's attention, and I've found I can do that by hitting a pan with a spoon, blowing a police whistle, or entering a room with my dress on backwards.

Of course it would be a lot easier just to say Bertha, but life isn't always that simple.

So when my son marries I'll remember to tell his wife that whatever she wants to call me is just fine as long as it isn't too formal, too flippant, too phony or too impersonal. And I never would have known that if it hadn't been for what's-her-name.

The Thank-You Note: He Shouldn't Have Done It 🐛 I don't know which is worse–receiving

a thank-you note from a child or trying to get him to write one.

Frankly, I'd hate to get the one my kid sent last week after his birthday gift deluge.

I mean, when his Aunt Charlotte opens that envelope, she's going to be looking for a letter, and what she's going to get is something that rivals Hemingway for short, clear sentences. After that, any resemblance to Hemingway is negligible.

"Dear Aunt Charlotte," he began. "Thanks."

When he brought this to me for final approval, I asked, "Aren't you going to say what you're thanking her for?"

"Naw," he answered, "she knows."

This remark brought forth a short speech from me on the importance of being earnest and an order to return to his desk and write something meaty and imaginative about the socks Aunt Charlotte had so generously sent.

He disappeared into his room and turned his radio up another twist for inspiration. I set the stopwatch. He was out in just under 47 seconds with another note. I've written better ones to my milkman.

"I'll tell you something, kid," I said, turning now to threats. "You'll never get another birthday present from anybody if you don't write a decent acknowledgment." He didn't look the least bit frightened. Pushing on, I added: "Do you want to grow up to be a lout?"

He thought a minute. "Will it keep me out of the draft?" he asked.

Sometimes it's better not to tamper with nature, so I let him send the note. He wrote three others, equally bad, and then settled himself down in front of the television with three bananas and a quart of milk.

"Sure makes a guy feel good to have done the right thing," he said, turning a banana-filled grin in my direction.

I wonder if being a lout will keep him out of the draft.

I'm No Child of Julia's 🍎 Some women
feel jealous when they watch Sophia Loren on TV, but I feel jealous when I watch Julia Child.

Do you know how I feel when my husband tells me my cooking is just like his mother's? You would if you had ever tasted his mother's cooking. The only thing she thaws completely before serving is the ice cream. You don't know what "cold turkey" is until you've experienced Thanksgiving at her house.

Not only are her meals bad; they're late. It takes her two hours to open the refrigerator. So you can imagine how I feel when my husband compares my cooking with his mother's. And it doesn't help any that my kids prefer things untouched by mother's hands—bananas, peanut butter, and TV dinners.

So when I saw Julia Child concocting a little French casserole she said was easy, I adjusted the horizontal hold and sat down to watch. Now is my chance, I thought, to find out the secrets of the saucepan. I too can win the lasting devotion of my family and make the poor girl who marries my son look miserable by comparison.

Well, Julia was only on for a half hour, but she did more cooking than—as my mother used to say—"you could shake a stick at." She not only cooked; she filled me in on all the little intellectual details, such as what the root word for scalloped potatoes is. I've forgotten what she said it was, just as I've forgotten how many tablespoons of cornstarch to add to thicken the wine sauce. I should have paid attention, but as I watched her excel, my jealousy grew so great that I began to concentrate only on derogatory observations.

For instance: every time she chopped up a scallion or a mushroom, she tossed the knife off-camera for somebody else to wash. She used at least twelve little mixing bowls and deftly swept them aside after emptying them. Who, Julia Child, is your dishwasher?

And she did plenty of tasting, but never once swallowed anything. How do I know she was using real food? It looked so perfect when it was finished, I'd swear it was papier-mâché.

There has to be a flaw in you somewhere, Julia, and I'll find it if I have to watch you every week.

Playing the
Old Match Game 🐝 Whoever is taking pencils from beside the phone is also swiping matches.

We have hot and cold running water, electric lights and indoor plumbing, but no matches. Man's earliest discovery is yet to be found around our house.

"Get the matches!" my husband screamed last Sunday as he stood beside the barbecue. I looked in all the secret places and finally found a book with three left–in the bottom of my purse.

I don't smoke, so they had probably been there for a year and a half.

Heroically, he struck them. They had as much fire in them as Elke Sommer's Uncle Henry.

"Go get the ones off the living room table," he ordered.

Five years ago a friend gave me a hand-decorated box of matches which we kept on the living room table until they disappeared–roughly twelve hours later. But my husband is afflicted with recollection of things past, and everytime he needs a match he imagines they are still there.

"They've been gone for five years," I said gently, not wanting to upset him.

It was too late. He had lost control of himself and was rummaging around in the laundry hamper.

"I think I left a book of them in my work pants," he said and, stopping suddenly, rolled his eyes like John Barrymore playing Hamlet. "Wait! What about the glove compartment?"

He ran out to the car and I followed him–having the consummate presence of mind to grab my coat and purse on the way out.

Of course there weren't any matches in the car, so I suggested he forget the whole thing and take me out to dinner.

We found a charming little place—with a book of matches on every table.

Home Movies: Nobody Wants To Get into the Act 🦋 When you watch those

television commercials showing life's precious moments slipping through the fingers of everybody who doesn't own a movie camera, you don't stand a chance.

I saw a tiny actress blowing out her four birthday candles and thought of the snapshots of my own kids' birthday parties showing them overexposed and cut off from the neck up.

"Listen," I said to my husband, "we really ought to have a movie camera so that we can record life's precious moments."

He turned toward me the way he does when he hasn't been listening and said, "Hmmm, yes, of course."

So I bought one. It's the kind of camera that any child can operate. We paid extra for that, but we shouldn't have, because we have a whole family of film makers now.

Usually, everybody wants to be in the movies, but at our house nobody does. Everybody wants to be the producer, director and exhibitor.

I lit the candles on my son's cake and said, "Blow those out for me while I record this precious moment."

"You blow 'em out, ma," he replied. "I want to use this super-eight zoom and get a close-up of your nostrils while you're inhaling."

He has seen too many art movies and isn't interested in realism. My husband is, though. He has the Walt Disney approach.

"Now, everybody line up on the lawn, sing 'Zippidy

Do-Da' and wave," he instructed as he wrenched the camera from our son's grip.

My daughter solved the dispute by announcing that she had to have the camera right away to make an experimental film for her communication arts class.

"Good," I said. "Take some footage of your brother blowing out his candles."

"No, no, mother," she said. "This has to be like a real movie. I'm going to the Colonel's and shoot people waiting in line for chicken. You know, slice-of-life stuff."

She tossed the camera strap over her shoulder and swung off down the driveway. The way the sun hit her blond hair was quite lovely.

"Look," I said to my husband, "there she goes to make her first experimental film. Doesn't she look cute. Run in and get my old box camera so I can record this precious moment."

Son Snares a Drum 🐝 The idea of playing a musical instrument appeals to most children, but the trouble is that today boys don't want to take up the harmonica. They all want drums.

"Listen," I said to the eight-year-old last week, "a harmonica fits nicely into your pocket. You could play for people at a moment's notice."

He was unmoved. He had the Christmas mail order catalog open to page 310 and was reading the copy aloud to himself, "Exciting beat of a TOM TOM . . . rustle of a SNARE DRUM . . . the full boom of a BASS plus brush and crash effects of a brass CYMBAL." The full-color picture beside this tantalizing blurb showed a male model with a big grin on his face apparently frozen in the middle of a paradiddle.

What chance has a mother got against that sort of thing?

But I tried. "You'd have to wait and wait for something that big," I said. "But I could run down to the drugstore and buy you a harmonica right now." For a minute I thought I had him, but desire won over immediacy.

"I'll wait!" he cried triumphantly.

"Now just a minute . . . " I began, trying to back him out of the loophole he had found, but it was too late.

"Oh, mom, thanks! Thanks!" he said. "I'll wait. I'll wait as long as three days if I have to. And I'll never ask you for another thing as long as I live."

That really got me. Just think, if I bought him the drums now, I could forget about getting him a surfboard when the time came and, eventually, a car of his own. That's a good deal any way you look at it, so I said okay.

He ran happily out to play, drumming his fingers along the woodwork as he went. And I couldn't help but notice that the kid did have rhythm.

I picked up the catalog and read the small print. The set of drums weighed 42 pounds and cost $288. Less per pound, actually, than a good steak. Maybe I could pay for it out of the grocery money.

Insurance Is the
Best Policy 🦋 For what is commonly referred to

in our time as "pennies a day," it is possible to insure everything in your home that plugs in or turns on.

If this news turns you on, it is probably because your washer overflowed while you were out shopping. When you came home and found your kitchen awash, your first thought was not how to get upstream after father's best shirt, but what it would cost to drain the living room and fix the machine.

Well, fret no more. With the proper policy, you can

now overflow, fail to heat, stop making ice, and even break down completely; it's all covered.

When my husband brought home our policy, I was skeptical. "It's just like when you go Christmas shopping," I said. "Salespeople take advantage of a man. If I had been with you, they never would have dared."

He put the policy away, looking the way he does when I refuse to clean a fish he has caught.

"It's only pennies a day," he said.

I was unconvinced. But three days later everything began to deteriorate. First it was the dishwasher. It just hummed instead of washing, and I couldn't have been more delighted.

"Guess what!" I said to my husband. "The dishwasher is on the blink."

"Great!" he answered. "Call the man."

I did, and he was in our kitchen for hours and hours. Any other time I would have been frantic—running into the other room to figure time, labor and parts while my blood pressure went up and my spirits went down.

But with our policy, I was relaxed and gay. "I hope it's nothing cheap," I said pleasantly. "We have coverage, you know."

"Lady, your whole heating coil needs replacing," he said gravely. I laughed and offered him a cup of coffee. I could tell he thought I was a wonderful sport.

The TV man was pretty impressed with me, too. One morning we couldn't get Mr. Wishbone. That may not seem like a big problem to you, but our six-year-old is dependent on him for survival.

Within minutes the repairman was there with the good news that it would cost a whopping $175 to bring Mr. Wishbone back into focus.

I kept my cool, flashed my policy and offered *him* a cup of coffee, too. And what if my automatic coffee maker should fail, due to the added strain of being bountifully cordial to repairmen?

Never fear. I think that's covered too.

My Potatoes Are Lumpy; Let Us Give Thanks 🦋 Every Thanksgiv-

ing, it dawns on me anew that I will never pull off a smoothly executed dinner.

I used to think it was because my table was too small or my roasting pan too big; but I corrected those things, and every year I still feel like Charlie Chaplin: helpless.

For one thing, the sort of kitchen help I get at a family gathering dinner is substandard.

Like my sister wearing her new white crepe dress with the bell sleeves asking if she can do anything. I hand her an asbestos apron and tell her to take the pie out of the oven, and it takes her fifteen minutes to get her sleeves arranged so she can open the oven door.

By that time the potatoes I'm mashing have begun to lump and the pie is smoking. I'm beginning to get a little nervous.

Four kids rush in to tell me they all want a leg. "Look," I say as sweetly as the season demands, "I'm cooking a turkey, not a centipede."

They exit, arguing loudly among themselves. Meanwhile, back in the family room, two relatives who haven't seen each other since last Thanksgiving are exploring the reason why. It seems they hate each other.

And don't tell me to plan ahead. Gravy cannot be made in advance, and gravy is important, because without it nobody would have anything to talk about. No matter what I do to my gravy, somebody always says it isn't the kind Great-Aunt Zelda used to make.

At first this sounds like an insult, but I have total recall, and I don't feel too bad. Aunt Zelda made gravy that looked like glue over cobblestones and tasted the same.

Time enhances memories–Aunt Zelda's gravy notwithstanding. So, some of my more sentimental relatives will undoubtedly reminisce again this year that "Zel's gravy was really something–remember all those giblets?"

And I will try to control the urge to tell them those giblets were flour lumps. After all, Aunt Zelda tried.

And any woman who plays hostess to her assorted relatives on Thanksgiving deserves to be remembered fondly. Who knows, someday somebody may remember my lumpy potatoes.

Mom Buys the Pants 🦋 Back-to-school

shopping for a boy entering high school is an experience I wasn't prepared for.

I mean, I can understand why he doesn't want to hold my hand when we cross the street anymore, but why should I have to walk half a block behind him?

"Ma," he said out of the side of his mouth, "get back!"

"Back?" I echoed, looking around. "What do you mean?"

At first I thought there might be a rabid dog loose on the sidewalk and he was trying to protect me.

"The guys. The guys are coming," he said.

Two harmless-looking boys ambled past us and exchanged mute greetings with my son. Boys of fourteen say hello with a quick lift of the chin and a brief closing of the eyes. My son looked up and down the street hurriedly to make sure the coast was clear and then ducked into a clothing store.

"Look," I said to him, "if this whole thing is too much for you, I could go home with my charge cards."

"No, it's OK," he said generously. "Just sit down in this chair here by the door and don't move."

I can remember when I said the same thing to him when he was three. He spoke to the clerk in monotones and disappeared into the fitting room with several pairs of pants that looked just like the ones he had on. When he came out, he handed three pairs to the clerk and walked over to a rack of shirts. He picked a purple Hawaiian print to go with beige cords.

Fourteen years of mothering is not easily suppressed. I stood up and inched my way toward the shirt rack.

"This brown Hawaiian print with the yellow pineapple would go a lot better with beige than the purple would," I whispered.

"Sit down," he whispered back.

Back in my chair, I picked up a magazine and peeped over the edge to follow the rest of his selections. Except for a touch of color blindness the kid has impeccable taste. And good timing.

"Mom," he finally said, "come here a minute. You have to sign for this." It's good to be needed.

Snoopy–A Dog to Remember 🐝 We have, living on our corner, the last of the old-time dogs.

He is a rock chaser, a cat charger and a street sleeper. Pure SPCA, he has not been hampered by feelings of inferiority because of his lowly background. He is, in fact, top dog in our neighborhood.

Other dogs look to Snoopy for behavior standards. The afternoon the pound wagon stopped to pick him up, two beagles and a poodle tried to get in with him.

He is first to tour the curb on trash night, and his

refuse inspection could easily qualify him for a job with customs.

It's not that Snoopy is a handsome dog, or even attractive. In fact, if you gave him a second glance, it would only be to make sure he is a dog. His torso is normal enough, but it is mounted on legs of different lengths. His front legs are short while his back legs are long. This unfortunate caprice of nature has doomed him to trot through life perpetually downhill.

Snoopy's home life is a canine's dream, as the mother of the family is under the impression that he hasn't eaten for weeks. She feeds him several times a day, but at the sight of food, the dog goes into such paroxysms of delight that the mother assumes the cat next door must have eaten his previous meal.

The father of the house professes to have no fondness for animals in any form, and his rejective attitude might have done Snoopy real harm had it not been for the four boys in the family. Among them, the boys have more than made up for any lack of acceptance. They have given a Gabby Hayes dog the confidence of Cary Grant. He carries his tail like a battle standard, and his gaze is steady and direct.

He's a dog's dog and his own master. As to winning over that father, Snoopy seem to be making headway. "Look at the way he crosses his little front paws when he lies down," said the father recently during an unguarded moment. "Did you ever see a dog do that before?"

Snoopy and I exchanged glances. I said, "No."

It was a lie, but with a dog like Snoopy, a girl hasn't got a chance.

A Time To Live
and a Time To Buy 🦋 The folder in the

mail said "Midsummer sale" in big, bold type, and I had
no trouble dropping it into my wastebasket.

The thought of a sale in mid or any other kind of
summer does not send my blood racing, though I am not
a woman who can easily pass up a regular $10.00 adobe
oven for only $3.99.

Indeed, I have been known to stand in line to burst
through department store doors all for the sake of a
98-cent potholder for 39 cents this week-end only.

But not, in heaven's name, in the middle of summer.
The middle of summer is a time when rat race gears
should shift into neutral.

Do not try to seduce me onto the freeways in search of
merchandise, Mr. Retailer. I am strong enough to turn a
deaf ear to your promises of a 30 percent saving on
famous bedding. I prefer to sit on my patio and contem-
plate the texture and color of a peach too beautiful to bite
into.

I'm not interested in new shoes at a saving. I'm patter-
ing barefoot through hose water right now to check on
the progress of my front lawn, which is mostly crabgrass
but still amazingly green.

And you will have to find another buyer for your $99.88
stereo entertainment system, regularly $169.95, because I
am prone on a chaise longue, eyes closed, listening to
bees, panting-puppy trots, birds' wings, and kids calling,
"Please, can we go in the sprinklers?" They are lovely
sounds, available in unison this month only.

Hurry home, Mr. Retailer, or to your nearest vacation
spot and take advantage of tremendous savings for your
memory bank. Stock up now while the supply lasts.

Please do not send cash. Just find a hammock or a hill

and ease yourself down–summer is a time for opening yourself to the warmth of the sun. A time to store it up, that warmth.

Live now; buy later.

Daughter's Gas– Her Tank Runneth Empty 🐛 It was

Mark Twain who said all children over twelve should be put in a barrel, fed through a bung hole, and not let out until they turned eighteen. As I quoted this to a friend recently, she looked surprised and said, "Why let 'em out at eighteen?" Clearly, she was a woman who had had recent contact with an eighteen-year-old.

I would have known it, had she not said a word, by the tic in her right cheek and the way she jumped at loud noises. My own eighteen-year-old has given me a case of sweaty palms and vertigo by announcing that she is ready at last to cut the silver cord.

"Mom," she said, "I want to meet my own expenses from now on."

"Yeah?" I answered, narrowing my eyes. "What do you mean by that?"

"Well," she continued, "you and dad can pay for my college and keep on making my car payments and everything but I want to buy the gas."

Encouraged, I told her that every little bit helped and that we would be delighted with her contribution to her own upkeep. Since then, she has been driving all over town on EMPTY. "Listen," I said to her, "your gas indicator is pointing below E. If you're going to buy gas, buy it."

She looked at me like I'd been reading her mail. "How'd you know where the gas indicator was pointing?" she asked. And I had to confess that I had started her car

30

in the driveway and checked on her gas supply out of motherly concern that she not be stranded on an off-ramp.

But suddenly I felt as if I were living her life for her–especially when she told me that only the day before she had put in $1.50 worth of gas.

"And you know, mother," she said slowly and patiently, "when you put in a gallon and a half the indicator doesn't move–it just trembles a little."

That makes two of us.

I'm probably the only mother in town who wishes her daughter would get tanked up. For Christmas I'm giving her a can of gas and a siphon whether she wants it or not.

And in the meantime, as the Irish blessing goes, may God hold her in the hollow of his hand, the road rise up to meet her, and the wind be always at her back.

Don't Light It, Dad 🐝 Once upon a time

Junior used to sneak out behind the barn to smoke. Now dad is the one behind the barn.

It all started with mass media and medicine. When medical researchers discovered that lives could be saved by snuffing out cigarettes, millions of hooked parents became the consternation of their children.

Warnings by the American Heart Association and the American Cancer Society did such a magnificent job that surveys show fewer and fewer young people are taking up the habit and 21 million adults have kicked it.

TV networks donated time for the messages, which otherwise would have cost close to $34 million.

Not bad; not bad at all.

But what about the poor devils who just can't throw away their ashtrays?

Take my husband. A year ago he tried to quit smoking

and started eating peanuts instead. Within three months his Steve McQueen silhouette had changed to Alfred Hitchcock. I had to kiss him sideways. And that takes courage–especially when a man has peanuts on his breath.

He was so irritable I had to ask permission to say hello to him.

Then one day, he broke down and went back to smoking. Even the dog wagged his tail. But now, with all the medical enlightenment hitting the whole family every time we turn on the TV, the poor guy has given them up again. He had to. It was the only thing his daughter wanted for Christmas. His son said, "Don't light it, dad. I want a father like other guys."

I even bought him a carton of sugarless gum as a substitute for the peanuts. But he is having a hard time of it. Twenty-two years of inhaling is not easily overcome. Just the thought of it makes me want a cigarette, and I don't smoke.

If he makes it, it has to be because of the kids.

"You don't think dad would smoke behind our backs, do you?" asked the nine-year-old last week.

"Of course not," I said.

But if he is out there behind the barn, I'll understand. Nobody is perfect. Not even Steve McQueen.

Wanted: Teen Sitter 🦗 During the years

when I was running down baby-sitters at the last minute and forking out 75 cents an hour to the girl up the street, I dreamed of the day when my kids would be old enough to baby-sit themselves. A movie and dinner out for my husband and me then wouldn't run into $17.

Life would be simpler, I thought, when I could say, "Dad and I are going to the show tonight. There's cold chicken in the refrigerator. Lock all the doors and pull the shades down." But, as in most situations viewed from afar, the cookie didn't crumble quite that way. What's happened is that my daughter's social life has eclipsed my own. At a blooming fifteen she has–as my grandmother used to say–"gentlemen callers."

"Dad and I are going to the show tonight," I said one night last week, and she smiled brightly. "Good! Freddie is coming over, and we can watch TV together." What's a mother going to say to that? Open all the doors and pull the shades up? A good beginning, but hardly a total solution.

It was then that I realized I had been pretty well off when I could hand over my parental duties to the kid up the street for 75 cents an hour.

When your daughter has a gentleman caller, you can't call a baby-sitter; you have to stay home yourself. But not home the way you think, all comfy in your PJs in front of the TV, but fully dressed in the back room.

"Don't you and dad hang around," she warned, "but come in once in a while so Freddie will know you are here." Just my luck to have a proper daughter. Instead of being allowed to go to bed early, I have to make periodic runs through the living room to prove my existence.

"Hi there, Freddie," I say as I circle aimlessly in front of them.

But Freddie is so entranced with daughter that he doesn't even notice my peculiar behavior.

And I may get even more peculiar if I don't get out of the house soon to a movie. I'd even settle for a quick walk around the block.

Call Your Dog 🐝 Whenever we leave town,

we take our two dogs to the vet's to be boarded until our return.

Sometimes it costs almost as much to leave the two of them behind as it does for us to go. But we rest easier knowing they are safe and happy.

Or at least we did until I read in the morning paper that a German zoologist, Dr. Joachim Poley, thinks vacationers are subjecting their dogs to "serious psychological disturbances" by heading for the hills without them.

But Dr. Poley doesn't just leave the dog owner hanging there–he has a few suggestions: before you go on vacation, Poley says, put your voice on tape and have it played to your dog every day.

Well, I don't know what kind of dog the good doctor has, but my dogs have taste. Higgins wags his tail when he hears Peggy Lee do "Fever," and Noche prefers Bach. They certainly aren't about to settle for a makeshift tape of me saying heaven-knows-what.

I could send a few records along with them–Sinatra maybe–but with both dogs on the phone all day, I doubt if they'd have time to play them. Because that was another of Poley's suggestions–call your dog daily on the telephone.

Very frankly, I'd be more worried about the vet's psychological condition if I were Dr. Poley. How is the vet going to hold up when the phone rings every day and it's me saying, "Let me speak to my dog"?

What are people around him going to think when he says, "It's for you," and hands the phone to a cocker spaniel?

Besides, nobody ever calls my dogs at home because they're rotten conversationalists.

Dr. Poley's final suggestion is that you leave behind in the vet's kennel a piece of your clothing, because dogs miss your smell as well as your voice.

Sorry, doctor, but I have obeyed so many TV commercials for deodorants that not even I know what I smell like anymore. A sweater worn by any other master would

34

smell as sweet. We are a roll-on society.

I don't know what to tell you doctor, except that I'm going on my vacation and I don't intend to call my dogs. Not unless I do it with a whistle.

Computer's Pet 🐛 If your child comes home

from school someday and tells you that his teacher isn't human, there is a good chance he will be right.

In Palo Alto, computerized classroom instruction is a reality for 135 grade school students. The father of the program, Dr. Patrick Suppes, one of the nation's top mathematicians, insists that the computer will never completely replace the old-style human teacher–but how can we be sure just what he has up his slide rule?

As surely as two and two make four, once a kid spends a year under the stoic, unobservant eye of the computer, he will not want to return to the all-seeing eyes of Miss Biddle. He will want to stay in there swinging, with that marvelous little piece of technology that enables him to learn his lessons and still remain the undisputed champion spitball thrower of the sixth grade.

It will take only a few minutes for the kids to learn that, along with daisies, computers don't tell. Teach, yes; but tell, no.

Can you picture a midmorning scene at the old schoolhouse two weeks after Miss Biddle has been turned out into the streets to look for work?

The computer has been installed in the approximate vicinity of Miss Biddle's old desk. It is humming softly, lights atwinkle, spewing information at the kids. Over in the far corner, Fat Eddie, one of the strongest students, has built an intricate structure made up entirely of school desks.

Perched on top of it we see Farley, one of the lightest

students, throwing chalk at the girls. The girls have taken refuge in a corner, and the rest of the class is busy shooting craps.

Only one boy watches the computer–and he has always had trouble adjusting to the group. After lunch the computer repeats the morning lessons, then repeats them once again before the final school bell.

Thus, the students absorb information in much the same way their elders absorb TV commericals.

The kids file out of school chanting, "The Battle of Hasting was fought in 1066. King Harold lost to William the Conquerer, yeah! yeah! yeah!"

And where is Dr. Suppes now, when we need him most? Why, out programming a new computer, of course. One that will send notes home to parents.

So far, he hasn't had much luck–the computer keeps saying, "Johnny has been very . . . bleep . . . bleep . . . bleep." It is at a loss for words, just as poor Miss Biddle would have been.

But Miss Biddle couldn't care less now–she is picking grapes somewhere and hasn't felt better in years.

Free Enterprising Boy
Is Expensive 🍎 My son is going into business

for himself. Usually, such a momentous decision takes place when the kid is around thirty-seven, but my boy is only nine.

He is completely materialistic in his outlook. "I want money," he declared as he sorted the forty-five envelopes of seeds he had sent for.

"That's just wonderful," I answered, relieved that he didn't want to take up the sitar and meditate for the rest of his life. After all, somebody had to follow in his father's footsteps and keep up the payments.

"Who do you think will buy my seeds?" he asked.

"How should I know?" I answered, which is the only sort of reply you can expect from a mother who has already put in a nine-hour day.

So he set out by himself in the cruel world of door-to-door. Surprisingly, he returned in less than two hours with almost half the box gone. I looked at him with new eyes. The kid has talent, I thought—must have inherited it from my side of the family. (I have a sister who sold mistletoe every Christmas to the tune of 25 cents a twig.)

But then, two weeks later, everything began to come into focus. First, it was the kid next door with the Girl Scout cookies. Then it was the boy down the street with the YMCA salted nuts. Throw in the chocolate bars for the high school drill team and the chances on the new car for the church and you come up with approximately the value of half a box of seeds.

As Al Capone would say, "It's all a matter of protection. I'll buy your boy's salted nuts if you'll buy my boy's seeds."

But then, that's a pretty decent arrangement any way you look at it. Heaven knows I'd a lot rather drive around town in a new car eating salted nuts than till the soil and sow those seeds.

Add on Angst 🐝 If you've ever added onto

your house, built a new one, or even completely redecorated, you probably feel the same way about it as I do.

Like childbirth, it is an ordeal but, once over with, well worth the anguish. Two years ago, when the last plasterer clumped out of my house—across the newly laid carpeting—I breathed a sigh of relief.

When he came back a week later for the scaffold he had

forgotten in the middle of the kitchen floor, I breathed another sigh of relief. Today, every time I see a plasterer, I breathe a sigh of relief.

Personally, I never want to see another paint sample, fabric swatch or giant key ring with 500 formica squares dangling from it. I never want to make another decision and realize, at 4:30 in the morning, that it was wrong.

When you're decorating, that's the hour you always realize you've made a mistake, and the only time you can correct it is right that very minute; and when you shake your husband awake and tell him, do you think he cares?

"Look," I said to him one miserable morning before the sun was up, "I don't think I'm going to like looking at that beige formica for the next ten years. I think we ought to go wild with sunshine yellow. Do you think the formica man has an answering service?" Rolling over, he groaned and looked at me as if he were trying to identify me.

The only time anyone will offer any kind of opinion is after the job is completed and it's too late. Then everybody has a friend who did what you did and lived to regret it. Either that or they will tell you they liked your house the old way–lived in. That's like telling a woman who has just dropped forty pounds she was more fun fat.

But if you're thinking of redoing your house, don't let me stop you. Go right ahead, only don't show me your swatches.

Making Peace With Thackeray's Letter Advice 🦋 It was

William Makepeace Thackeray who said, "Make your letters safe. I never wrote a letter in all my life that would commit me."

He must have been some pen pal. His being so definite about being indefinite may have influenced letter writers for all time. It certainly looks that way.

Take those school notices, written by principals, that float home to parents every once in a while. "The faculty has reevaluated the lunch hour for children in grades one and two with the recommendation that the time be shortened. In our judgment the time change will be beneficial for your child."

The only benefit to my child I can imagine is that the teacher who watches the lunch benches will be able to get a grip on herself sooner if the little hellions file into the classroom fifteen minutes earlier.

Another fifteen minutes with those kids and she might attack them all with a tetherball pole.

The time change is fine, but why don't they say what they mean?

The next time a friend writes me a letter asking where I bought a Christmas gift and whether I mind if she exchanges it, I hope I have the courage to write, "Yes, I do mind. If I'd thought you were going to exchange those socks, I'd never have bought irregulars, and now you are putting me in an awful position. But since we are on the subject of gifts, for heaven's sake stop crocheting those antimacassars for my birthday every year. They don't go with my Spanish decor."

It may be the end of a beautiful friendship, but it might also be the beginning of a beautiful correspondence.

How delightful if, by return mail, I received the following: "You've opened your last antimacassar. I hated doing them anyway. Why don't we just forget your birthday like you did mine last month?"

Love letters are not usually written straight from the shoulder.

"Mabel, I will love you until the day I tire of you. Our love is as perishable as the next couple's. Tonight, when I fall asleep, I will dream of nothing because I am beat from running that bulldozer all day."

And her letter to him might be equally frank. "I read your letter today during my lunch hour, and I know what you mean about being beat. I hope you propose soon so I can quit lugging those trays and sit around an apartment all day watching TV."

When two people like these are joined together, it is because the mailman could not put them asunder.

And I do wish corporations would stop writing me letters as if I owned controlling interest instead of four shares. When I get thick packets of proxy instructions full of legal-sounding terms, it makes me very nervous.

If I'd wanted to be under such a strain, I'd have bought 50,000 shares. Why don't they just send me a little note saying not to worry, they'll make the decisions. Because they are going to anyway.

Thackeray started the whole thing, going on and on about safe, noncommittal letters that skirt the truth. If he could look back from wherever he is, I'll bet he'd do things differently if he had a second chance.

Sorry, Mr. Thackeray, there is no return address on your envelope.

A Mother's Grimm Tales 🍎 Nicholas

Tucker, a British psychologist, is warning mothers to go easy when it come to frightening youngsters with nursery stories; they may be too grisly.

From the inner London education authority, Dr. Tucker said even illustrations may be repulsive, "like the forest scene in Walt Disney's *Snow White* in which his trees sprout clutching arms and hideous faces."

True enough, I suppose, but I don't remember my mother telling me any grisly nursery tales. She stuck to facts–like what would happen to me if I didn't stop biting my nails. I didn't need an illustration to picture that ball of fingernails somewhere between my duodenum and my small intestine. Her powers of description were astounding.

Mother also had a large store of horticulture information. Swallowed orange seeds sprouted within two weeks and bore fruit in the spring. I didn't have time to worry about Snow White's forest; I had trees of my own to contend with.

So far as sinister characters go, such as the scissor-man who cuts off thumbs in Heinrich Hoffman's *Struwwelpeter*, Dr. Tucker needn't worry about my having any hang-ups because of that tale. At seven I'd never even heard of the scissor-man.

It was the man who took the Lindbergh baby who had me worried. Kidnappers were very big in the thirties, and mother read everything on the front page aloud at the breakfast table.

"Will he get me?" I would ask, and mother would try to put me at ease with, "Heavens, no. Kidnappers want rich children."

What she didn't know was that I had $1.45 hidden under the edge of my bedroom rug, along with a picture of Bruce Cabot. Could any kid be richer?

And mother never frightened me with threats and stories of the Big Bad Wolf. Not when she could get her point across by using actual persons.

"Do you want to grow up to be like your Aunt Roma?" she would ask whenever I failed to clean up my room. Aunt Roma had twenty-seven pairs of shoes under her bed, some of which were occupied by small living creatures. Talk about grisly.

But I wish Dr. Tucker luck in his campaign against scaring the daylights out of kids. As for the scissor-man, now that I know about him, I'll keep my doors locked.

Guilt and Anxiety
at the A&P 🦋 If indulged in to any great extent,

reading psychology books can be very unnerving. When I
was in high school I used to read first aid books, and I
managed to imagine I had everything described, from
shock to snakebite.

Then I grew more mature, graduated to Karen Horney,
and realized that one does not have something simply
because one reads about it. One has something because
one really does.

Take basic anxiety. Oh, have I got that! I can't give you
the scientific definition because I have trouble retaining
any sentence over twenty-seven words—one of the sym-
toms of basic anxiety. Also one of the symptoms of being
slow-witted. But anyway, if you get the urge to abandon
your car on the freeway during rush hour, you might
have basic anxiety too. Or maybe you have the same
feeling I do at the supermarket check-out stand. It's Friday
night and you only went in for a bottle of aspirin, but you
discover that Friday night at the supermarket is swinging
singles night. There you are in line holding your bottle of
painkiller and wearing your rump-sprung pantsuit and
rubber thongs, while all about you it's party time.

Everybody in front of you has gay things in shopping
carts, like wine, thick steaks and sour cream. You duck
out of line and grab a 69-cent bag of gumdrops just to
prove you have a little fun left in you. Classic basic
anxiety.

I'm no more secure in the supermarket earlier in the
week, either. Only instead of anxiety, I have guilt. It's
4:30 and I dash in to pick up something quick for dinner
after a hard day shopping for new clothes. I am dressed
to the nines, having worn everything I bought out of the
store.

42

Exhausted as I am by my effort to rival the cover of *Vogue*, I only feel up to cooking one of those awful dinners that come complete in a plastic bag: all you do is toss it into a caldron of boiling water.

But who is in front of me at the check-out stand? A woman in a rump-sprung pantsuit and rubber thongs who has all the stuff in her cart to go home and make a four-layer chocolate cake from scratch. Where was she when I needed her Friday night?

She looks at my plastic bag of dinner and my impeccable attire, and her eyes are cold.

Talk about guilt and frustration! Lady, believe me, on any other day of the week I'm just as big a slob as you are. Maybe even bigger.

All in all, I think I'd rather be in shock or have a snake bite me. I wonder what I did with that first aid book.

Earth Art Moves Indoors 🐛 Have you

heard about "earth art"? It's an avant-garde movement in which certain innovators return to nature by filling elegant galleries with mud, grass, dust and gravel.

For a woman who has always hankered after an original van Gogh, earth art may be just the answer. Frequently I hint around about wanting van Gogh's sunflowers–I'd even settle for a Picasso sketch–but I keep getting bath powder and subscriptions to the *Ladies' Home Journal* instead.

Good art is simply too expensive. But now, with earth art, I might be able to have an original right away. All I have to do is relax and stop telling the kids to wipe their feet every time they come into the house. I'd have works of art all over the kitchen floor and original earth art in all traffic areas.

So much for mud. As for dust, my living room is

already pretty arty, and conditions under the beds are priceless. I have enough going for me behind the refrigerator right now for a one-woman show.

Funny, all these years I thought I was careless, and it turns out I'm just gifted. If my housekeeping gets any worse, people will be asking for lessons.

Even a good housekeeper can get with the earth art scene if she has a boy between two and twelve. Small boys have sand and gravel in their shoes, pockets and pants cuffs. What's more, you can count on them never to empty into the wastebasket where it might go unappreciated.

I suppose I'll always want that van Gogh, but it is a comfort to know that until we can afford it, there is always earth art. And I intend to increase my collection from its present state of small to an eventual really big mess. And I think I can do it, too. I may not know much about art, but I know when I need to vacuum.

Pencils, Please 🍎 I don't ask for much. With

my deck of credit cards and the usual assortment of material burdens, I manage to get along fairly well.

Except for one thing: I don't have a pencil. A sharpened pencil, easily accessible, is about as hard to find at my house as a spinster at a rock festival.

I had a pencil once, but word got out. "Gimme a pencil!" shrieked my son one afternoon in the middle of my nap.

"What for?" I shrieked back, because there was no sense in letting him see where I had it hidden unless he really needed it.

"I wanna poke a hole in the side of my mattress," he answered.

Now, I ask you–what would you say to a kid like that?

Exactly. And I said it too, only it turned out he was supposed to poke a hole in the side of his mattress as part of a science report for school. At least that's what he told me.

By the time I had given it a second thought, he had my pencil. Along with science, my son is interested in karate. He can shatter a pencil with one swift blow. I have the pieces to prove it.

But pieces can be sharpened, and if you can write with a half-inch stub, all is not lost. Unless you have to write more than three words, in which case you run out of pencil and patience at about the same time.

My birthday is approaching, and I've been quizzed about what I'd like. I keep telling everybody to get me a pencil–get me a box of pencils–but they only laugh. I've almost reached the point where I'm ready to go out and buy one.

But who ever heard of anybody buying a pencil? You get them from insurance agents, husbands who bring them home from work, and old dance cards dug out of memory boxes. In the meantime, until somebody gives me one, I'll be taking phone messages with a bobby pin dipped in coffee.

Is Your Living Room Saying Nasty Things About You? 🐝 Dr. Edward Laumann, associate professor of Sociology at the University of Michigan, has some big news for all of us about our living rooms.

After visiting and interviewing over a thousand families around the country, Dr. Laumann and his colleagues have come to this disturbing conclusion: a sophisticated person can easily categorize his neighbor just by taking a good look at the other fellow's living room. And if you think Dr. Laumann is talking about housekeeping, forget it. This guy's approach is scientific, so it won't do you any good to vacuum before he rings your doorbell.

He takes away points if you have your TV in the living room. Dr. Laumann says a television that hasn't been relegated to the den or bedroom is a hallmark of the "lower classes."

Drat! Couldn't you make an exception just this once, doctor? Didn't you notice my set is in a bookcase surrounded by many volumes? Doesn't that prove I don't watch TV all the time? I read. Ask me a question about Nancy Drew or the Hardy Boys–go on, I dare you.

Because I need the points, doc, I really do. I'm not going to score at all on my carpeting. It's wall-to-wall and solid color—a sure sign of being "newly prosperous" and a person who "likes things seen in magazines." You can say that again.

And if you had tripped and slid over those throw rugs I had for 15 years, you'd understand why I turned to *House Beautiful* for help. I had one rug in my hallway that was swifter then Hans Brinker's silver skates.

You say that "old rich" have wood floors showing and use area or scatter rugs. Did it ever occur to you that they can also afford to have their legs set more often?

And really, Dr. Laumann, when you invaded all those living rooms, couldn't you have had the courtesy to let sleeping dogs lie? You say, "Other working-class living room signs are the presence of dogs, especially mutts and the commoner breeds. Afghan hounds and Borzois are all right in the upper-class living room; French poodles are OK for those who are just 'making it.' "

Come on. If I could lift it, I was about ready to move my TV to the bedroom. I might have even given some thought to ripping out the carpeting. But that dog bit did it. You lost me there.

Rejecting a dog of questionable lineage because his presence tips off my social status would be like gassing my grandmother because she prefers black-eyed peas to cherries jubilee. My dog, and everything else, stays.

And I hope you have the courage to ignore your own findings and resist keeping up with the Gettys. If not, Dr. Laumann, the next time you and your Borzoi sneak into the bedroom to watch *Laverne & Shirley*, I hope you both trip on a throw rug.

Time Out for Failure 🐛 Today when a

man comes home and asks his wife, "What did you do all day?" they both know it's a joke.

They both know darn well what she did: everything. Even if his wife didn't tell him, a husband could hardly help but guess. She has dishpan hands, accelerator foot, sewing machine stoop and new-baby nerves. But she is smiling. Not only is she smiling; she has done her hair a new way.

Along with all those other things, our housewife is also suffering from magazine syndrome. She spent her 15-minute lunch hour on a slant board swallowing a peanut butter sandwich uphill and reading one of those devastating little articles so prevalent in today's women's magazines–articles that don't warn a woman about failure; articles that assume she has already failed. The titles include "How to Combat the Other Woman," "Why Do Husbands Stray?" and other assumptions that make an ordinary woman feel as if she simply isn't with it unless she is in the middle of a crisis. Or, worse yet, that there is something going on she doesn't know about.

No wonder she trains that winter curl in such a spring-like way; she is trying to win the old boy back from whoever might have him. Even if it takes 45 minutes– about all the time she can spare between chores.

Too bad friend husband doesn't read the same articles so he could know what's expected of him. As it is, he is above suspicion. Which brings up the ultimate question: Can a woman find happiness today if she already has it?

Of course. All she has to do is cancel her subscriptions.

Keep the Change ❦ Now that belts are back in style, I can get one of those money-changers streetcar conductors wear.

If you've ever had a kid ask you for a popsicle and given him a quarter with orders to "bring back the change," you know, as well as I do, that you have about as much chance of seeing your remaining 15 cents as Hugh Hefner has of making Eagle Scout: very little.

But with a money-changer I wouldn't have to ask that classic question: "Where's the change?" and be told my debtor had treated himself to a stopoff at a pay toilet.

I don't care how little or how much change a kid has left, he will somehow manage to get rid of it. Take lunch money. For 40 cents the school cafeteria serves a noontime meal that is wholesome, hot and balanced–what a bargain! But unless you have the exact change it will cost you whatever you hand your child.

I just rummaged through three chair cushions and the bottom of the washing machine looking for four dimes so I wouldn't have to give my son a five-dollar bill. I'd have packed him a lunch, but I was out of everything except two paper plates and a jar of peanut butter. (And don't think I didn't toy with the idea of making him a sandwich out of that.)

All I could find in the chairs and the washer was 27 cents and a straight pin which rammed itself under my fingernail with such exquisite pain that I momentarily lost control of my senses and gave him the five-dollar bill.

After school I was waiting for him with my hand out, but I needn't have bothered. He told me he had paid for the math book he'd lost, replaced a student-body card he'd lost, and paid off a dollar bet he had lost to a boy who had been lurking by the bicycle racks every day after school for two weeks waiting to collect one way or another.

I think it was Socrates who said nothing is certain but change. He must have had a belt with a money-changer on it.

Toast Clear Vision with New Glasses 🐝 My oculist is not the sort of

man you'd expect him to be. He coaches on eye tests.

"Listen," I said to him as I sat forward on a tiny stool in his office squinting at an eye chart, "I can't see that bottom line at all. It's just a blur."

He pushed the stool, which was on casters, a bit nearer the chart. I blinked and peered.

"E, F, B?" I asked.

"Try P, B, C," he whispered.

"Why should I?" I said irritably. "What good will cheating here do me when I'm trying to read the price tags at Saks?"

He smiled indulgently.

"I'm telling you, doctor," I continued, "I need glasses. I've lied to myself for two years, but I'm sick of reading *Lad; a Dog* just because the print is big."

He threw back his head and laughed. "Getting to be that age, eh?" he said. Apparently, advancing age and impending blindness were sources of merriment to him.

"Look," I said, grabbing his starched lapel, "give me a pair of glasses or I'll go to the five-and-ten and buy a pair for 49 cents that will ruin my eyes. Think of your Hippocratic oath."

Finally he opened a tiny drawer filled with sample lenses and grudgingly slipped a few into a pair of empty frames he had affixed to my nose. With the fourth set the bottom line suddenly jumped out and I read it.

"Doctor," I exclaimed, "I can see!"

But his sense of the dramatic was flawed. Clearly, he had not seen Bette Davis in *Dark Victory*. Where was his merriment now?

Dourly he scribbled a prescription for the optometrist and looked at me gravely.

"Now when you get these glasses," he said, "don't wear them all the time."

"I won't," I lied. "Honest Injun."

And, in a way, I've kept my promise. I never wear them unless I'm looking at something. And if I want to read *Lad; a Dog* I always take them off.

Caution:
Charging Children 🐝 Montgomery Ward,
second only to Sears, Roebuck as the Great White Father of retailing, has come up with a credit card for kids.

It's a sales promotion that's enough to strike terror into the hearts of mothers everywhere. Because a mother knows perfectly well that when she gives her child a dollar to run to the store for a loaf of bread, not only does she kiss the kid good-bye, but the change as well.

Kiddie credit is enough to make strong fathers weep and weak fathers strong. I mean, it's one thing for a man to liberate his wife so she can get a job that pays as much as his does, but when his ten-year-old starts spending both paychecks, that same man will dry his hands, snatch off his apron, and run to the bastions.

Montgomery Ward, get hold of yourself. When you issue those 5.4 million kiddie credit cards, you are tampering with the psyches of mothers and fathers who have been on the brink through 2 A.M. feedings, Parent-Teacher Association jamborees and Little League picnics. Don't push us.

Wards, I don't care what you say about a phone number on that credit card where I can be reached. After my kid has run through your tempting store, I'd just as soon not hear from you. What would we have to say to each other?

"Madam, your child is here in our credit department and has found thirty-seven items he's crazy about. What do you say—yes or no?"

To a phone call like that I'd say: "There must be some mistake. I have no child—what you have there is a bankrupt midget. I'd advise you to get that merchandise away from him any way you can to protect your overhead."

And don't tell me to come in and pick him up so I'll buy a refrigerator and some lawn furniture. It's your ballgame, Montgomery Ward, and I wish you luck.

You're going to be up to your escalators in bankrupt midgets, and it's all because you didn't give their parents enough credit. And I don't mean Charge-All.

Big-City Bends 🦋 I can remember when life
was simple and all I had to worry about was getting stuck between floors in an elevator.

Now, heaven help me, I have to cope with subterranean parking. And I don't mean one level down–I mean those supersubterranean burrows that have to be there if a building is going to shoot up seventy stories into God's blue sky.

Subterranean parking has given me a new dimension in fear. I know what it is to want to get out of an airplane right away–even if it's over Kansas City–and I am familiar with the need to whimper softly when a kid hands me his pet king snake to hold as a special treat.

In short, I am an experienced chicken. But have you ever had the desire to back up on a subterranean down-ramp? It is not a pretty feeling.

I had followed big yellow arrows deeper and deeper to levels where, I'd hoped, there might be a slot for me to park. I was down so far they'd run out of primary colors for level identification. I was between burnt orange and lavender levels when I began to worry about getting the bends, and decided I'd like to back up.

I stopped and looked in my rearview mirror. Solid cars behind me. I rolled down my window and asked the man in the car behind me if he would please back up a little so maybe everybody would get the same idea and we could all go home and take a nap.

He honked. I rolled up my window and proceeded downward. You've come a long way, baby, I thought, and you're going farther still.

It was on burgundy level that I finally found a slot to park, got out and took detailed notes on where I was: "Burgundy level, section B, row H, space 24, just this side of the river Styx."

I'd been underground so long I felt like a mole. Fortunately, the garage floors had been laid out for the survival of idiots, and by following a yellow vinyl path, I stumbled onto one escalator after another until I was finally deposited on ground level.

I took a big deep breath. Smog. It was good to breathe it again.

Order in the Schoolroom or Else 🐾

The campaign to end corporal punishment in public schools makes me wonder if the campaigners have something else in mind—like maybe capital punishment.

I mean, if teachers in junior high schools aren't allowed to use the switch, maybe they could be allowed to throw it. A classroom with thirty-two seats wired with 600 volts would be an innovation in the field of discipline. It could bring a whole new meaning to the term current events.

"Well, Johnny," a mother would say to her son on his arrival home, "what happened at school today?"

And the boy would answer, "Plenty. We had a current event. Freddie got 15 volts for sassing the teacher."

And any kid who tried to hit her could get the full 600 volts. What a way to teach thirteen-year-old boys to stand up when a lady principal enters the schoolroom.

I think teachers will go for the idea, and any parent who protests could be made to do two hours' volunteer work in the school library. There, such parents would quickly realize that their kid may be perfect, but he is sharing the library with 65 thugs. Where returning a book means throwing it back at the guy who threw it at you. And overdue means he had it coming to him.

The most lenient of parents will soon subscribe to the old adage on capital punishment: "Spare the rod and spoil the child." Colt 45, that is.

Once order is restored in public schools, the challenge of real education can begin. Foreign languages can be taught—kids will be saying "please" and "thank you" fluently.

And the voice of the teacher, bless her, will again be heard in the land.

Rattlesnakes Are Just Plain Folks 🐛

Every year the warmth of spring brings forth slender blades of pale new grass, fragile blossoms—and rattlesnakes.

Sorry, if I made you spill your coffee, martini or whatever you might be sipping this time of day, but it was unavoidable.

Because what I have to tell you is urgent: Harvey Fischer, Los Angeles Zoo curator, is asking us to please stop molesting rattlesnakes. If you haven't already spilled your drink, I'm sure it's down the front of you by now. I mean, how's that again, Harvey? Me molest a rattlesnake?

I don't even argue with the guy at the market who puts rotten strawberries in the bottom of my carton. When the driver in back of me honks during a red light, I think Zen.

And you're telling me to lay off rattlesnakes? Come on. Next to tooth extractions without novocain, I like rattlesnakes least, but I'd never tell them. I wouldn't do any of the things you warned the public against doing.

You said, "Don't stomp them." Count on me. You said, "All the rattlesnake wants is a warm rock to sun himself, a good meal and maybe a mate."

I can understand that, and I'll do everything I can to make him happy, short of introducing him to my best friend: let him find his own dates.

Harvey also says the rattler is "just as scared as the person who encounters him." This may be true enough, and I'll try to remember it.

But please, if you have such rapport with rattlesnakes,

54

Harvey, spread the word among them that we innocents who meet them on paths and among the rocks shouldn't be molested either.

Tell the little fellows that all we are looking for is a warm rock on which to sun ourselves, a good meal and maybe a mate. If you can make yourself as clear to them as you have to us, I'm sure everything will turn out fine.

In the meantime, I think I'll take a little snakebite preventive–two fingers of Scotch over a warm rock.

Yoga Your Way and I'll Go Mine 🐞

Yoga, according to my paperback book on the subject, is a Hindu discipline aimed at training the consciousness for a state of perfect spiritual insight and tranquillity.

If there is one thing I need on Monday morning when the washing machine is making funny noises and the steam iron is spitting rusty water at me, it's a state of perfect spiritual insight and tranquillity.

So I signed up for a course in basic yoga. My classmates were attired in leotards and sitting in the lotus position when I rushed in out of breath and fifteen minutes late–very un-yoga of me.

But the teacher was prepared for such western slip-ups and motioned me to a mat where I sat Indian fashion and closed one eye, keeping the other one open in case I might miss something.

By the end of the lesson, however, I had closed it–having learned three relaxing exercises and a deep-breathing method which made me think I'd missed my calling.

Clearly, I was cut out to be a guru. Here were exercises I could do standing still. Breathing, which I have always done well, was considered an accomplishment.

And the teacher's instruction to go directly home and meditate was the kind of homework assignment I'd been waiting years to hear.

"Get away from me, kids," I said to my children when they came home from school. "Mommy is meditating."

"Can we watch?" they asked.

"No," I said. "This is strictly between me and my consciousness."

They disappeared, but the dog came in and sat down in front of me and gave me a long look. Then the phone rang.

And the kids giggled from the hallway where they were making elaborate plans to crawl in on their stomachs to spy on me.

Now I know why yoga students head for the Himalayas. Nobody can get to them there.

The Celebrated Empty Nest 🐝 "I am

suffering," said my neighbor, "from the empty-nest syndrome."

"Yeah?" I said, drawing nearer for a closer look at her. "What's that?"

"It's when all your kids have gone and you feel useless and unneeded."

She went on to tell me she had discovered her malady one day while sitting out on her patio in the sun reading a magazine. In the magazine was an article about middle-aged women and how useless they feel when they are no longer needed to wipe noses and be sure the dog is let out on time.

"Not until I read that article," she said, "did I realize how miserable I was.

"I had two kids in college, and I'd been spending my days reading, shopping and going out to lunch with stimulating friends. Can you imagine? I did all those things when I should have been in bed resting my syndrome."

"Are you kidding?" I croaked. "Your syndrome will take care of itself. You don't know when you're well off."

She rose on one middle-aged elbow and gave me a long look.

"Ya mean it?" she said.

"But yes," I said. "Just because you don't have a kid around the house who can count to a thousand and then ask if you want to hear it backwards–that doesn't mean you can't find joy elsewhere. You can compensate for those unforgettable mornings when you got up at 6:30 A.M. to pour bowls of sugar puffies and pack lunches of peanut butter sandwiches.

"Although those tender moments are gone forever, you could force yourself to stay in bed and read the editorials. You could get up when you want and take a bubble bath. It might be hard at first, but try."

She brightened somewhat and blinked back a tear.

"Then I'm not washed up?" she said.

"Stop talking like a detergent commercial," I told her, "and start identifying with the one that says 'You've only just begun.' Now's your chance to start calling your husband by his first name again instead of referring to him as 'your father.' "

She smiled. She was trying to remember it.

"Bill," she said softly. "His name is Bill."

I think she's going to pull through.

Hot Tips from a Mini-Tycoon 🍓 One of my best
friends was completely wiped out by the current stock market drop. Lost everything he had–$12.32.

I hated to see it happen, since he is only eleven, but I think he may make a comeback. Because, if ever there was a mini-tycoon, he is. He's the kind of kid who could sell you a melting popsicle on your way into the Ice Follies.

When he makes collections on his paper route, he has change for a fifty. He reads the label on the vitamin bottle to make sure it says USP–which I always thought was just the initials of the guy who bottled them. He is, in short, one smart kid. That's way I couldn't understand how the stock market could do him in.

I thought he knew all the angles. His parents don't take a morning paper, so he comes over to my place to check the market everyday. It was the morning he took off his glasses and covered his eyes with one hand that I knew something was wrong.

"I've gone down the tubes," he said briefly.

"Oh, Scott," I said, "how did that ever happen?"

He helped himself to a piece of cinnamon toast and gave it some thought. "Well," he said at last, "I think I bought in too soon. I should have waited until it hit bottom." That's an observation I think even J. Paul Getty would agree with. See what I mean? The kid has a head on his shoulders.

"Listen, Scott," I said, edging a little closer to him, "what do you think I should do with the $47 I've been saving? I mean, is there something you'd invest in if you had your $12 back?"

He helped himself to another piece of cinnamon toast and gave it a little thought. Finally he said, "Yes, as a matter of fact, there is."

I pushed the plate of cinnamon toast toward him and said, "What?"

He looked at me carefully to make sure I was worthy of the information, and then he told me. "Mrs. Rudy," he said with all the aplomb of Paul Newman, "how would you like to be let in on the biggest buy of the century?"

I fell off the breakfast bar stool and said breathlessly from the floor, "Tell me!"

"It's stationery," he said.

"Stationery?" I croaked.

"Yes," he answered. "I'm selling it. For $47 you will never have to reorder again."

I believe it kid, I believe it. Have another piece of cinnamon toast and keep your eye on the Dow Jones—just like you, it has its ups and downs, but it will endure.

It's Your Move, Madam— Enjoy It 🐝 We are going to move soon, and the moving company sent me a helpful little folder telling me how to do it.

But the poor guys have everything all wrong. That's men for you.

They have a paragraph headed "Packing Day" that tells you to "hold sufficient food and cooking and eating equipment for evening and breakfast meals."

What kind of planning is that? I packed my frying pan as soon as our buyers gave us their deposit. I had every pot and pan and all the knives and forks in the trunk of the car two weeks before escrow closed.

Then I pulled a few strands of hair down into my face, increased my breathing rate and said to my husband, "I'm worn out from all this packing. Absolutely exhausted.

"The worst thing is, I can't cook those wonderful meals of mine for you and the kids because the kitchen is all torn up."

He told me to lie down with my feet higher than my head, and then he opened the refrigerator and looked in. He found a half-eaten can of dog food and a bottle of milk that had turned to cottage cheese.

Returning to my side, he took my hand and said: "Brace yourself. We'll just have to eat out for awhile."

I bit my lower lip, averted my eyes and replied: "Whatever you say, dear."

Somehow or other, I managed to get up off the floor, put on my new dress and choke down dinner.

The folder contained other curious instructions too. One said: "Reconcile your checking account and close it." What are they talking about? My checking account hasn't been reconciled for fifteen years. As for closing it, how could we do that and still pay for all those dinners out?

The jet set may have their fun, but there's no reason why you can't groove when you move too. Just don't read those helpful folders.

Give a Man a Bag He Can Open 🌱

It is a curious thing that men can get to the moon yet have such a hard time opening a bag of potato chips.

I have seen young men, old and middle-aged men all reduced to utter helplessness when confronted with a sealed waxed bag.

Little boys too, only they aren't yet so self-conscious. They don't hesitate to punch a hole in the side of the bag and catch what they can before it hits the floor.

Pickle jars are different, of course, because they come under the heading of muscular strength. What woman hasn't called helplessly from the kitchen, "Come here, dear, and open this jar for me," and then stood by in awe as the big brute twisted off the lid like it was a toothpaste cap.

If a man can give his wife little else, he can give her the gherkins. But potato chips are another story, as are those sealed cardboard boxes of breakfast cereal.

Last week I stood by as long as I could one morning while my husband scratched and clawed at a box top of puffed oats, and then I thought, To heck with it.

"Do you want me to help you?" I asked, and he handed me the box. I had it open in less than a second. It was not an easy moment to live through, and I had no pickle jars handy for him to save face with, so we both ate our puffed oats in strained silence until he couldn't stand it any longer and said:

"You know, the cereal company printed the wrong directions on that box top. They said pull up and it should have been punch in."

"Yeah," I said between mouthfuls. "Same thing with the potato chip bag."

"You noticed that too?" he marveled.

"Sure did," I lied. "No way to get into a potato chip bag short of dynamite."

He relaxed over his cereal and munched on. I just hope he never realizes he's not man enough for Granny Goose.

Gimme a "K," Gimme an "I," Gimme a "D" 🐝 I know as much about

football as I do about baseball, which is to say nothing. I always thought Babe Ruth was a child movie star and the Rose Bowl was a nursery in Pasadena.

But now things have changed. I've bought a stadium cushion, a thermos and a pair of binoculars. And every Friday night I'm sitting on the 50-yard line a half hour before the kickoff.

I don't read the sports page, and I still think a hand-off calls for medical attention–but what's a mother to do when her daughter is a cheerleader? She does exactly what the mothers of the band, the drill team, the first-string team and the second-string team do—she turns out to watch her child.

A high school stadium is one part kids and two parts parents. The kids are the ones who watch the game and cheer. The parents are the ones who watch the kids and cheer.

Only last Friday, while I was waiting for the band to finish a particularly long march, a woman in front of me turned around and said, "That's my boy on the tuba."

"You don't say," I replied, fanning myself with the program, but there was no stopping her.

"And my girl is the one with the glockenspiel," she continued.

Clearly she didn't realize the importance of the cheer-leaders, because she was still watching the band even after they stopped playing. She missed the great yells taking place not three feet in front of her.

"F-U-M-B-L-E it!" shrieked my daughter as she jumped up and down in that cute little green skirt I had pressed two hours before.

"F-U-M-B-L-E it!" she repeated. Simply adorable.

But can you believe the parents next to me were impatient for half-time activities? The mother confided to me, "This year's drill team is the best ever! Our daughter is the captain."

Of course. But pay attention to those yells, lady, or I swear I'll close my eyes all through half time.

Go ahead, precious—yell. Mother's watching.

The Kite of Knowledge 🍎 Buying a

book for a kid should be done very carefully. I found that out by bringing home a book I thought would enrich my child's mind.

It was full of facts. The moment he thumbed listlessly

through it, I knew he wasn't as interested in enriching his mind as I was.

That was a fact the book neglected to include. The flyleaf promised children a thousand and one answers, but what about the kid who doesn't want to pop the question?

"Did you know," I said to my boy, "that aeronautically speaking, a bumblebee cannot fly?" I asked this question after arming myself with the reasons on page 108.

My son looked at me with fascination. Encouraged, I filled him in on all the little things about a bumblebee even a bumblebee's best friends don't know. Then I sat back to receive the wild acclaim I felt entitled to as the smartest mother on two tired feet. But what I thought was fascination on my child's face turned out to be curiosity.

"How come your eyes look that way underneath?" I had the answer without even checking the index. "Because," I said, "I am pooped. Those are bags."

Curiosity satisfied, he scampered out to play. But what am I going to do with all those leftover facts? Throw them away with the leftover brussels sprouts? Never.

I read the book myself, which is only fair since I selected it. Now I know that the sun's surface is 11,000 degrees Fahrenheit and that the Potawatomie Indians used to eat skunks.

As for my boy, his current source of enlightenment is a broken kite which he is repairing for a friend.

"Did you know," he asked me, "that Kenny can't fix his own kite?"

"What a clod!" I answered, but he corrected me. "No, that's okay, because I can't fix my reel—so he's helping me with it. Kenny is a neat guy."

The fact that Kenny is a neat guy may not be as startling as the eating habits of the Potawatomies, but it is nice to know. And especially nice when you have found it out for yourself. No index needed there.

Do you suppose the bookstore would take that book back? I only read it once.

Food for the Thoughtless 🦋 There's no

way to drive up to a plastic clown and tell him what you want for lunch and not feel ridiculous.

I don't care how hungry you are, when you roll down your window and yell, "Give me a biggie-burger, fries and a large orange," it does something to your dignity.

So usually I try to take a couple of kids with me. But this does something to your dignity too.

I mean, kids love drive-through hamburger stands, because they like to say funny, alarming things to the plastic clown along with giving their orders.

It isn't easy to face the guy at the hand-out window after three kids, who are now hiding on the floor of the backseat, have said, "Three hamburgers, two malts and four hot apple turnovers. Hey, clown, I love you and this is a stickup."

I've gotten a lot of weird looks in my time, but the ones at the drive-through window hold precedent. It doesn't do any good to explain, either, because the boy can't hear you over the roar of his cash register.

The best I usually manage is a Gallic shrug. But it hurts when the boy hands me my change and a bagful of food and doesn't even say, "Have a nice day," like everybody else does.

I really don't think they want my business at the plastic clown. If I come in alone they only make 35 cents, and if I bring the kids with me they get very uptight.

Or if they don't get uptight, I do. Because sometimes the kids decide not to say funny, alarming things and hide, but to argue instead about who will give the order to the plastic clown.

The way they go on about it, you'd think it mattered. I have seen faces flattened, tongues rolled up and shoved back into mouths, and body blows delivered which would decommission Muhammad Ali.

Then, when the fittest has survived, he can't make up his mind. "Hurry up," I'll tell him. "The clown can't wait all day."

And the kid will answer, "I'll have, um . . . let's see, um . . . ," but the plastic clown smiles on and on.

Maybe that's what really bothers me about him . . . he doesn't have a breaking point.

Sleeping Over, and Over, and Over 🦋

"Sleeping over" is an expression I never heard as a child.

When I was growing up, people never stayed overnight unless they were visiting from another town or their house had burned down. But my boy has slept in more local beds than George Washington. And his friends have "slept over" at our house so many times the neighbors think we have foster children.

And that's OK with me: the boys are great kids, and I've always wanted two more children anyway. Besides, having a child from another household in our midst gives my husband and me something to measure our own behavior by.

One twelve-year-old philosopher announced at our dinner table that it was definitely a big mistake for him to push his father too far.

"Yeah?" I inquired. "What happens if you do?"

He laughed at my naïveté and said, "Well, if I bug him he sends me up the stairs the easy way–through the air."

"Through the air?" I asked.

"Yep!" he replied. "With a karate chop. He has his red belt and that's better than a black one." Or even a leather one, I'll bet.

After that, we found it easier to tell our son to get his feet off the breakfast table and be quick about it.

Then there was the boy who had a three-second conversation with his mother when he called to ask if our 200-pound dog could accompany our son on his overnight stay. The boy hung up so fast I thought he'd been disconnected. "What happened?" I asked.

"She said no," he replied, and it did my heart good to know there were mothers left who still knew how to say it.

"No," I said several times aloud to myself. "No." And I'll be ready the next time our boy wants to camp out under the offramp on New Year's Eve.

But there is one hitch to sleeping over, and that's toothbrushes. Once one goes out of the house, kiss it goodby. At 89 cents a brush, twice a week, it comes to roughly $7 a month—or the equivalent of 700 one-cent stamps. Think about it. It will drive you crazy.

But then there is always the compensation of the forgotten toothbrushes the other boys leave behind that you get to keep. I had just noticed that the brush I was using had a plastic giraffe on the end.

"Hey!" I called, my mouth full of foam. "Whose brush is this?"

And my son answered calmly and logically, "Oh, Paul left that for you because he used yours when he took a shower in your bathroom because sis was in my bathroom for three hours."

Of course. How silly of me to ask. But do me a favor, will you, kid? Next time you leave me a toothbrush, make it blue. Green looks simply awful with my wallpaper.

Pizza in the Afternoon 🦋 The diet con-

fession story is taking the place of the love confession
story.

Pick up any women's magazine and you'll find a
lengthy article about how Jane, just an ordinary woman,
managed to overcome her magnificent obsession with
chocolate cake or anything else she could lay her hands
on.

"When my husband left for work in the morning," a
typical passage will read, "I tried not to think about the
bowl of leftover spaghetti in the refrigerator, but it was no
use. I waited until the kids were outside playing, and
then I ate the whole thing. No one knew, because I
broke the bowl and carefully wiped my mouth. But that
afternoon I went back to the refrigerator and killed a leg
of lamb I'd been saving for company.

"That's when I knew I needed help. It was raw." Then
the reader goes with Jane through the agony and anguish
of clandestine gluttony. Stolen pizzas, furtive Fritos and
tremendous lunches in small, out-of-the-way cafés.

In the end, of course, Jane realizes that her real happiness lies not in a bed of lettuce smothered in Roquefort
dressing, but in the arms of Fred, her adoring husband.
Fred forgives her for the 200 pounds she has put on, and
she bravely shoves aside the extra eight meals a day she's
been eating–a sadder but wiser girl. Together, they resolve
to live happily ever after and never mention the wooden
spoon she bit in half during those mad and capricious two
years of gourmet gallivanting.

That's what comes of giving up our Victorian mores.
Sex has come out of the shadows and is now as wholesome as mom's apple pie. Mom's apple pie, however, has
become a no-no. Which only goes to prove, I suppose,
that guilt is here to stay–any way you slice it.

Dial "M" for Mother 🐝 I got the most

extraordinary phone call the other day. It was from Spain.

At first I thought it was my friendly neighborhood sex maniac. I had the sort of connection the police department warns you about–silence, followed by heavy breathing. "Hello!" I shrieked, and then: "I know you're there. Say something or I'll hang up."

But what I thought was heavy breathing must have been the tide or something, because all the way from the rocky coast of Malaga came a lovely, pockmarked "Hello" from a most devoted friend.

At the time, my kitchen–where the phone is located– was filled with milling children. I waved my free arm at all of them and, assuming a half-crouching position, opened my eyes to their fullest, which I hoped would convey my need for silence and solitude. Apparently the kids thought I was doing an imitation of John Barrymore, because they all drew nearer for a better look.

Clapping my hand over the mouthpiece, I hissed, "Get away! Go eat all the popsicles. Get away!"

They were fascinated. "What's the matter with your mother?" asked one of the brighter children as he scrutinized me carefully. But my son was busy passing out the week's supply of popsicles and didn't answer.

From sunny Spain came the faint announcement: "We just finished dinner at La Fonda–it's 3 A.M. here."

"I wish I were there," I yelled, and nobody could have been more sincere. "Can you hear me?" I shouted, picturing my voice rippling along the transatlantic cable as fish cocked their gills at the vibration.

"Hell, yes," came the answer, "You're just as loud as ever."

"Good!" I said, and then a strange thing happened. I was at a loss for words. I couldn't think of anything worth saying over an ocean. I mean, you don't tell

somebody in Malaga that the man who was going to fix
your washing machine pump didn't show up. Or that
your daughter is getting new rims for her glasses. It has
to be big news or nothing.

Apparently not much was happening in Malaga either,
because I kept hearing that tide. Finally my friend said,
"We miss you." And I, now surrounded by curious kids
eating popsicles, answered, "I miss you too." And we
hung up.

I sat down in the nearest chair and said to a red-headed
boy I'd never seen before, "Go get me a root beer
popsicle."

Munching it, I repeated to myself, "Spain. All the way
from Spain."

But I had lost my audience. They were outside playing.
What a great time for a call from Paris.

Ho-Hum,
Call an Ambulance 🐛 A San Francisco

woman was hospitalized recently because she simply
couldn't stop yawning. She is the victim of an unusual
but minor thyroid condition which caused her to yawn
every 15 seconds.

Don't look now, lady, but I think I've got it too. And
don't let anyone tell you it's your thyroid.

The newspaper story I read said your doctor was about
to send you home as your yawns had tapered off since
you entered the hospital. Wouldn't you think that would
have told your doctor something?

If I could go to a hospital, I'm sure my yawns would
taper off too. But sitting around home, there's just no
letup. There are certain things a housewife has to put up
with that she can't help yawning over.

Take phone calls. If a woman isn't married, a ringing phone could mean she has finally brought Steve McQueen to his knees, but to a married woman a phone's ring is sheer boredom.

It might be Gloria Wellright. You know her–she hasn't had a disaster in her family for 300 years. She doesn't call to let you know everything is OK–she calls to let you know everything is perfect. That includes her husband, her kids, and even her husband's mother. Try that one on for yawns.

Then there is the phone call that gets you in the middle of stripping the varnish off Great-Aunt Zelda's ninety-year-old chest–if you will pardon the expression. There you are, caustic paint remover eating through your rubber gloves into your cuticle, when the phone rings.

The caller asks for you by name. He sounds like the school principal, so you answer him as sweetly as anyone could whose fingernails are dropping off.

But it isn't the school principal–you should know by now the only word you get from him is mimeographed.

It is the salesman from your local cemetery who wants to know if you'd like to buy a plot. It's the third time he's called this week, and you begin to wonder if your doctor has told him something he hasn't told you. It's tiresome, that's what it is.

Ho-hum. If I didn't know better, I'd think it was my thyroid.

Identity Crisis for Mother Cabrini 🌿 There comes a time during a child's late

adolescence when a mother is required to be seen and not heard. Just ask my daughter.

"Mother," she has said, "I am fond of you, and I want

you to feel free to keep doing my laundry, cooking and vacuuming up the price tags I throw on the floor–but keep your opinions to yourself, because I am in the middle of what Erik Erikson calls an identity crisis."

A lot she cares that I'm in the middle of the same thing. I mean, I used to think I was Harriet Nelson with a touch of Mother Cabrini, but lately I've been feeling like Harpo Marx.

It isn't easy for a mother whose tongue has been figuratively torn out to let her daughter know that going out in the rain without an umbrella will result in rheumatism during later life. Or that parking tickets, unpaid, bring subpoenas and possible incarceration.

But I manage. Harpo rolled his eyes a lot, and so do I. The groan is also a useful means of communication. The groan, combined with a hand to the forehead, followed by a short gasp, can tell a kid plenty, but gestures will never replace a mother's words. Only yesterday she found that out.

"Mom," she asked, "where's your charge card?"

I stood before her mute, lips working, searching for the right words. "Come on, I'm late," she urged. I rolled my eyes toward my purse and jerked my thumb in the direction of the table on which it lay. She thought I wanted her to put on a warmer coat.

I tried again, and she thought I was warning her to fasten her seat belts. Finally she pulled me over to the sofa, sat down beside me and said how about a cup of hot coffee and a little chat–just the two of us. It was like the intimacy between an interrogating officer and the guy who won't tell what he did with the body. But it worked. She got her charge card and I got my voice back.

"Keep it under $20!" I called after her.

Maybe Harpo Marx with just a touch of Mother Cabrini.

Lunch Bench Barter ❦ Packing a kid's

lunch is more of a challenge than you might think.

My nine-year-old knows exactly what he wants, and it's the same thing every day: a peanut butter and jelly sandwich, twelve cookies, two cupcakes and seven caramels.

Of course he doesn't get anything like it. If I packed that sort of lunch he'd have beriberi, rickets and pernicious anemia.

I give him things like ham and cheese sandwiches, fruit, carrot sticks, and a small raisin-filled cookie. He carries this to school like a nice, obedient boy and promptly exchanges everything in the bag for a peanut butter and jelly sandwich, twelve cookies, two cupcakes and seven caramels.

I know because I got a full confession from him after I found a mashed caramel in his back pocket. It seems he is the king of the lunch bench wheeler-dealers.

"Mom, don't be mad," he began. "You don't know how hard it is to get rid of the stuff you give me. Carrot sticks are really tough to unload."

I tried to tell him what would happen to his bone marrow and his major league ball career if he persisted in his pursuit of cupcakes and caramels. "Do you want to pass out at first base?" I asked.

"Aw, ma," he said, smiling sheepishly, and I quickly checked his teeth for new cavities.

"I mean it," I continued. "You are to eat what I pack for you."

But I strongly suspect lunches are still changing hands every noon. A mother knows.

Somewhere in that school is a boy who is getting stronger and more solid by the day—on my kid's lunch.

I just wish there were some way to let his mother know. She's probably worried sick about all the candy and cupcakes she thinks he's eating.

What's in the Stars Is
Hot Gas 🦋 I can remember my grandmother read-

ing her horoscope before it was the thing to do.

"Well," she would say, "the sun is in my fifth house, and you know what that means." Of course I didn't, so she would fill me in on the year's coming disasters. I always wondered how she had the courage to go on, knowing what a long, tough haul it was going to be.

As I grew older, I figured grandma's horoscope reading was a little like her cooking—she had faith in it, but not many other people did. Now I have discovered horoscopes not only are still around, but are really coming into their own. People have become maniacal about things zodiacal.

Signs of the zodiac are found on cocktail glasses and sweat shirts and dangling from pierced ears. The astrologers are forecasting in morning and evening papers so we will all know exactly what the stars have in store for us.

Just when I thought I had grandma's number, I find myself wondering what's happening in my fifth house again.

But worse than what's happening in my fifth house is what may be happening in my fifteen-year-old daughter's astrological life. My paper carries a forecast with a special little paragraph called, "Teen Dating Hints." Last night's hint read: "After 10:30 tonight atmosphere undergoes change—from passive to active."

Is that any kind of message for a nervous mother to read who is waiting for her daughter to come home? I'm not sure what my lunar position is, but I think it favors jumping to conclusions. What else can I do when the Teen Hint goes on with "Leo gets starry-eyed tonight. Fine night for athletic contest."

Hold on there, Leo. I have my own forecast for you: "The moon is overhead,which means it is after 10:30 and high time my daughter was in her own house–the fifth one from the corner."

I'll admit it doesn't sound half so exciting, but I'm sure my grandmother would have believed in it.

Coffee for a Connoisseur? 🦋 My husband's idea of good coffee is not in keeping with what he preaches.

For years he has told me, patiently, that the best wines are carefully aged. He has instructed me not to shake the bottle and disturb the sediment before pouring.

Only last night he read the label on the dinner wine and exclaimed, "Ah, 1959. That was a good year." I have listened well; I have the message. And I have carried this training over into my coffee perking.

When I pour his morning coffee I am always very careful not to shake the pot, so the loose grounds will stay in the bottom where they belong. But what does he ask me?

He asks me, "When did you make this?"

"Last night," I answer–which is, I realize, nowhere near 1959, but it's a start. So why does he cover his eyes with one hand?

I do the best I can for someone without a European background. I mean, if he wants me to come to the breakfast table wearing a coffee cup around my neck on a chain and give him a drop of coffee to taste before I pour a full cup, he will simply have to find another woman.

I'm just a plain, ordinary American housewife whose coffee is only one day old. But heaven knows I try. This morning as I poured a particularly dark brew for him, I tried to bring a little continental touch to an otherwise crushingly suburban breakfast.

"Ah, Thursday morning," I said. "That was a good day."

He pushed the cup and saucer away with one finger, and I couldn't have felt worse if he had slapped me across the face with his glove.

I held my grounds.

"This coffee is fresh day before yesterday," I cried indignantly, and he went right on reading the sports page. I guess some husbands are just harder to please than others.

But it is beginning to dawn on me that when it comes to coffee, there is no vantage in vintage.

Give Us a (Station) Break 🦋 The other
night as our family sat watching TV commercials, again and again these vital messages were interrupted by the news.

Most commercials are only 60 seconds long, and that isn't really enough time to cover the entire area of the average American's insecurities.

Sure, in 60 seconds I can find out which paper towel will hold the most water and which tissue gives me twenty extra sheets, but I also have to think about whether or not my sandwich bags are waterproof.

I have to decide which cleanser gets the deep-down stains out of my sink, and this kind of information just can't be thoroughly explored in 60 seconds.

My daughter needs the breath information so she can stay kissable. My husband needs the antacid pitch for his stomach, and we are all getting fed up with having some sobersides burst in and tell us what is happening around the world.

Can a viewer with tired blood really give a damn? Who

wants to listen to a weather report if the air in his own house smells like cabbage?

We need to know which aerosol spray will help us right here at home. People over sixty-five can't concentrate on news of Social Security reforms if their dentures keep slipping in public and are full of stains from red wine. I say let's get these advertisers together and have feature-length commercials. At least an hour and a half of uninterrupted, information-packed help for the ordinary family who would like to become more involved with the world about them but can't—because of thinning hair, headache, constipation, BO, indigestion and corns.

Once we get ourselves and our houses in order, maybe then we can turn to the outside world. Maybe then we can say, "Yes, world, I care about you and I'm interested in making you a better place."

Until then, let's have more in-depth commercials with real emphasis on smelling nice.

Sonny, Can You Spare a Dime? 🦋 When it comes to money, I have no luck at all holding onto it.

I have a way of making a dollar do the work of 12 cents. My husband is generous enough, but he knows by now I am perpetually in need of a loan. He knows it, but I hate to admit it.

So rather than tell him I have blown my weekly allowance on such frivolous things as haircuts, Scout jamboree tickets, sneakers and food, I have gotten myself into real trouble.

I'm involved with one of those loan sharks you hear about. Only the one on my tail is really merciless. It all started innocently enough one day while I was out strolling with my nine-year-old son. "You know," he said, "money is only paper." Right away he had my attention. Not only because I thought the remark pretty astute for a kid, but I just happened to need four dollars.

"You said it!" I exclaimed. "How about a loan?" He was very accommodating, mainly because he is one of the reasons I'm in debt to begin with. He has all kinds of money because he never spends any.

His money isn't in his pocket—it's all in the bank.

"Sure, mom," he said. "How much do you need?"

It all seemed so easy. He gave me the four, and before I knew it, it was a quarter here, a dime there. . . . Then he asked for it all back–suddenly. "Now wait a minute," I said. "I owe you $32.11. You'll have to give me a little time." His eyes narrowed and his offhand manner vanished.

"I need it," he said. I tried everything–even Portia's speech–but he wanted his money. "Why don't you just ask dad?" he said.

"Because," I answered, "I don't want your father to think I can't manage on what he gives me. You know how girls like to show off."

His eyes narrowed even more and he said, "Oh, I get it. OK, I'll give you a few weeks. But if I don't empty the wastebaskets or take out the papers, don't tell dad." Blackmail, pure and simple.

I still owe the kid $5, and he hasn't emptied the wastebaskets or taken the papers out for six weeks. His sister has been watching all this with deep compassion. "Mom," she said, "if you need $5, I can let you have it."

But I was too smart for her. "One more word out of you," I said, "and I'll let you have it."

Facts Can Be Dangerous 🐝 A Universi-

ty of Tennessee professor, Dr. Charles Helvey, says the
world is facing another serious form of pollution–too
much useless information.

I could have told you so, doc, but nobody listens to me.
As far back as 1952, when my husband and I moved into
an apartment so small the bed popped out of the couch, I
have been aware of the problem. "Listen," I remember
saying to him, "can't we get rid of some of these books
full of useless information?"

I didn't mind finding a spot for my thesaurus and *56
Ways To Cook Leftovers*, but his copy of *How I Made the Sale
That Did the Most for Me* and *Calculus for Beginners* were
what I considered pollutants. But no, he insisted on
keeping them. "You never can tell," he would say.
"Someday you might want to read them."

I'd rather curl up with appendicitis than a book on
calculus. I'd rather read the fiber content on a pillow label.

But I found places for those books in 1952, Dr. Helvey,
and you can find places for your useless information, too.
If you are newly married, try storing those books in the
oven. I did, and for a year and a half nobody was the
wiser. Sooner or later, of course, you'll want to start
eating and you'll have to empty the oven.

But marriage is full of adjustments; and you may find,
as I did, that books you never want to read can be used
for other things. Thin volumes may be used for stabilizing
table legs. Thick books are good for flattening envelopes
that have warped after being steamed open. (Not that
you'd open anybody else's mail, doctor, but you've got to
admit it's a lot more exciting than *Calculus for Beginners.)*

And, finally, there is great comfort even in books you
don't want to read, because they never have to be
watered; you don't have to housebreak them; and when
they are on a shelf in your living room, people think

you've read them.

So try to live with that useless information, doctor, as I have these last twenty years. And if it should get to be too much for you, try putting those books back in the oven and turning it up to broil.

Cleaning Up Is Hard To Do 🐝 A

funny thing happened to me on the way to the car wash: I got a spot on my car.

It wasn't a very big spot, but it was stubborn, and the boy with the damp rag was adamant when he said, "Lady, this here car's got a spot on it."

"I know," I said, twisting my purse nervously and looking around to see if anybody had heard him.

It was the second time I'd brought in a dirty car to be washed and I think he remembered me. He never even listened to my explanation, he merely snapped his towel at my hubcaps and slammed the car door on my ankle– which I had neglected to draw in quickly enough.

I make things tough for the dry cleaner, too. The spotter there writes little reports on cards and hangs them around the hanger tops of every article of clothing I pick up. They read: "We have done everything possible to successfully clean this garment, but the stains are oxidized and are aged in the fabric."

Aside from making me feel like the biggest slob in town, these little notes make me feel guilty too. I have done terrible things to my blue sweater. I have stood by and permitted my family to do mayhem with mustard on everything they own. And I have the guts to take these clothes, soiled as they are, to a cleaner. Flog me; I confess all.

There are days when I think almost everybody is on to me.

Trash day, for instance. Have you ever had your garbage rejected? Until it happened to me, I always felt that my garbage was as good as anybody else's. I had the usual middle-class stuff: high-protein leftovers, vodka bottles, and a couple of boxes from Saks thrown in to give the whole thing class.

Then one day the city wrote me a note, which I found tucked inside the ravaged carcass of a chicken–a carcass I never would have looked at twice except it was in front of my house for two weeks, along with five barrels of trash.

The note said my garbage was in the wrong size container, had no lid and was improperly tied. If I wanted to fool around with regulations like that, I would have mailed it. Today, if it's service you want, simply look in the Yellow Pages–under do it yourself.

Good Morning America Yourself! 🥚 If you are wondering if you are a

"night person" or a "morning person," come on over to my house sometime and watch me make breakfast.

I'm pure night person. Those of us in this fix cannot begin to tell the rest of you what it's like, but on behalf of the night person I would like to make a request of the morning people.

Please, for heaven's sake, all you sure of foot and clear of eye at 6 A.M., do not flaunt it. I have a husband who can get up at dawn and eat pork sausage and fried eggs while telling me, as I sway in the chair next to him, what a gorgeous sunrise he saw while I was trying to find my way down the hall and into the refrigerator.

"You have to glimpse it at just the right moment," he will say, shoveling in the eggs, "or you might as well just stay in bed." I try not to think about that word bed and ask if he would like more toast. To my horror he says yes. It is not an easy task to make toast when your arms are asleep and three quarters of your brain is still involved with the fascinating dream you had the night before. You may ask why I bother to get up at all. It's training.

My mother was a morning person, and every morning while I was growing up, she appeared at the foot of my bed, fully dressed, and announced, "Hot breakfast! I've been up for hours." Then she would give me the weather report and a rundown of news from the morning paper. I may not have had television as a kid, but I had mama. And today, when my alarm rings, her example of good, hot breakfasts is hard to ignore. So I get up and walk into my closet for my robe, only it isn't a walk-in closet.

"Time to get up," the kids will call, "Mom just hit the door."

But I do get up. And what does it matter if I fix breakfast with my eyes closed? By tonight I can say to my husband, who will be nodding in his chair, "Johnny Carson's on. He's gorgeous, but you have to glimpse him at just the right moment or you might as well go to bed."

A Boy's Room
Is His Rat's Nest 🐛 My boy's decision to go

to camp this summer has made me very happy. It means he will have an opportunity to learn woodcraft, independence and comradeship. He might even have a transcendental experience, though heaven knows I'm not the sort of mother to pry into his personal affairs once he gets home.

But let's not talk about when he gets home. Let's concentrate on that wonderful week he'll be gone—and how I will manage, somehow, to fill the empty hours.

While he is having all those opportunities, I'll be having a few myself.

For one thing, I'll be able to go into his room with a trash barrel, a rake and a Flit gun. When he is home, that's sacred territory. The last time I disturbed his pile of comic books, which I considered a fire hazard, you would have thought I was rummaging in the Gutenberg papers.

"Don't touch my April issue of *Wild Adventure*," he screamed, jumping off his bed for the first time in a week.

"Why not?" I asked. "It looks the same to me as the May issue."

"Well, it isn't" he howled. "There's a coupon in it I'm gonna send in so I can learn to throw my voice."

If there is one kid who doesn't need to throw his voice any farther, it's him. But a mother always hesitates to stand in the way of a child who would like to do better.

It's the same thing with the pile of clothes in the northeast-corner of the room. When he's home, I can't touch them.

"Why don't you hang that nice nylon jacket in your closet?" I will ask him.

"Because it belongs to Eddie Jenkins," he replies.

"Then return it to him."

"I can't. He moved to Florida."

"Then let's give it to the Goodwill."

"He's coming back next year."

That corner is a complete boys' ready-to-wear department—all of it unclaimed. But I don't dare take action while my son is home. What if he should tell? Not all those kids are in Florida.

But this week I'm going in there. Over the top! Geronimo! By the time my boy gets back from camp there'll be nothing in his room but a bed, a chair, and a copy of *Huckleberry Finn*. And if he says one word to me, I'll throw my voice at him.

Almost Alone at Last 🐝 Next to an

empty ironing basket, I thought the nicest thing that could happen to me was having someone invite both my kids to stay overnight.

Nobody would be crazy enough to ask both of them at once, but I hoped that occasionally–like the eclipse of the moon–they would be invited simultaneously by separate families.

That's what I'd call real luck. At least that's what I thought I'd call real luck until it happened to me a few weeks ago.

When the nine-year-old rushed in the back door and breathlessly asked if he could please stay overnight with the kid up the street, I paused just long enough to give my decision punch.

"Yes," I finally said, "if you clean up your room first."

He set about it, knowing it was backlash, but he was desperate to get out from under his own roof. He found socks under his bed he hadn't seen since he was two and a half. But that was about all I got out of it.

It seems the kid he was going to spend the night with hadn't eaten yet and it was almost six o'clock. "Can Stanley eat dinner with us?" asked my son. I don't know why, but I just figured my kid would eat at Stanley's. "Of course," I said gaily. (Stanley was standing there.) But I wondered how I was going to cut a chicken leg in half. I began to butter bread frantically.

It was no good. Stanley would have to have at least six chicken legs to sustain that Pop Warner physique.

I ran out to the garage and hit the accelerator–almost running over my daughter in the driveway on my way to the market.

"Mom!" she shrieked. "Terry is having a slumber party tonight and I'm invited."

I saw a light at the end of the tunnel. If I could just

stick it out, they would both be gone by 7:30–leaving my husband and me alone for the first time in sixteen years. Suddenly, I felt shy. "Yes," I yelled through the car window. "Yes! Yes!"

When I got back to the house with the six chicken legs, all was pandemonium. "He can't have my sleeping bag, can he?" cried my daughter.

"Stanley only has one bed," countered my son.

"Now wait a minute," I said, thinking of that glorious evening of privacy. "We can settle this."

And I was right. By 10:30 we had it settled. Stanley had eaten, I had driven five miles to borrow another sleeping bag, and my husband and I had dropped our son off at Stanley's. But there were six girls who had no way to the slumber party, and guess who picked them up and delivered them.

That's right–the honeymoon couple.

But we were home by 10:30. And then the phone rang.

"Mom," said our nine-year-old, "I want to come home and go to bed."

He wasn't the only one.

Yes, Sir, That's My Sitter 🦋 Sometimes
getting a baby-sitter is more trouble than it's worth.

Baby-sitters, like night-blooming jasmine, must be picked in their prime. Prime is between the ages of fourteen and sixteen. Before fourteen, the ingenue you leave little Freddie with may take his security blanket away. After sixteen, baby-sitters have a way of being busier than you are on Saturday nights.

So you find a nice, wholesome girl between fourteen and sixteen. But have you any idea what makes her so wholesome? It's the eight meals a day she eats. And all those tidbits between meals–just to hold body and bikini

together. By the time you buy the sitter her snack supply,
who can afford to go anywhere? At $1.50 an hour and all
she can eat, it would be cheaper to hire Johnny Carson to
sit with the kids. They'd be sure to like him.

As it is now, they hate everybody who's available. "Not
Janice," wails the six-year-old. "She's so mean."

The six-year-old thinks anybody is mean who makes
him go to bed before midnight. But you call Janice
anyway. You don't think Janice is mean—not until she calls
you 20 minutes before you are ready to leave and says
she has a sore throat. Then, she is not only mean but the
product of an inconsiderate and downright depraved family.

Then you remember she has a little sister who might be
able to fill in. Suddenly the family doesn't look so bad.
The kid sister is fourteen, pushing fifteen; and since you
already have your eyelashes on and a six-month supply of
candy bars in the cupboard, you call her.

She is delighted, and before you can say "Don't eat the
marinated mushrooms" she is on your doorstep. Not only
is she on your doorstep, but when you come home five
hours later she is on your bed—dead to the world.

The six-year-old lets you in, with the happy announcement that he just loves Janice's sister. And no wonder.
She has made it possible for him to watch the late, late,
late show undisturbed.

Good Night, Sweet Sister 🦋 My sister

has been suffering from an energy crisis for years.

As far back as 1965 she was turning out lights to save
energy—hers. She slept so much my mother thought she
was in a coma.

I won't say she was lazy, but any woman who likes
cookies because they are easy to lift, any woman who has

been upholstered twice because she wouldn't get off the sofa, could use a little pepping up.

And now she, like the rest of us, has been cautioned not to drive faster than 50 miles an hour unless it's an emergency. She doesn't drive at all unless it's an emergency.

The last time I drove with her, she went so slow that pedestrians were passing us. The driver in back of us didn't honk, he fell asleep at the wheel. Gas rationing doesn't worry her—she's still on her original tankful.

For years she has scolded me about my reckless driving—doing 45 on the freeway. "Ya wanna get yourself killed?" she'd scream, holding onto the door handle and watching for a chance to jump free. And the only reason she didn't jump was that she knew she'd have to walk home. That's out of the question for a woman whose shoe soles are like new.

That's why she won't be turning her thermostat up: she'd have to stand up and walk over to it. So when I heard about the energy crisis, I knew just whom to consult.

"How do you manage," I asked her, "to stay so unhurried, so indolent, in today's high-speed society?"

Stifling a yawn and rubbing one eye with her fist, she confided: "It's easy. Lots of TV and cutting back on my vitamins."

I'd been doing just the opposite, which only goes to show you that sometimes the best of intentions can be ruinous to our national welfare.

I just wish my sister would stay awake long enough for me to tell her what an inspiration she has been to me.

Help Yourself: Don't Eat ❦ I am long-
ing for the good old days when the only thing a woman

had to worry about finding in her food was calories, or
when an occasional story in the newspaper reported a
lawsuit brought against a candy company for including a
mouse in a box of fudge.

Far greater horrors await today's eaters. The food itself
is now suspect. A new book by Ruth Winter bears the
title *Beware of the Food You Eat*. It contains everything you
never wanted to know about food and were afraid to
think about. Information on chemical additives, food poi-
soning, inadequate inspection, pesticide adulteration, botulism and salmonella deaths. How about that for discourag-
ing second helpings?

Come to think of it, I'd just as soon forget the whole
meal. And I wouldn't think of having anybody over to
dinner for fear of being arrested for attempted murder.

A lot of people felt that way about my cooking long
before the food furor, so why should they have any more
faith in me now? After all, a woman who can't boil water
isn't very likely to properly disinfect the vegetables, is
she?

My fish would probably contain so much mercury the
guests would have to shake it down before eating it. But
there would be no worry about who had to do the dishes,
because my meal might be their last.

If I had any leftovers it would probably be guests in the
living room the next morning–fixed in rigor mortis and the
objects of frantic searches by anxious relatives.

"I can't understand it," I would alibi. "I served them a
little canned soup, and they suddenly lost all interest in
the story my husband was telling." He's had them fall
over with boredom before, but never with botulism. With
boredom they're always up in time for dessert.

The whole thing makes entertaining rather risky business, and it doesn't do much for family nutrition either.
Now, instead of nagging my children to eat eveything on
their plates, I'll have to police them to be sure they don't.

"Lay off that spinach," I'll say. "How do I know what's on it besides sand?"

Tricks Your Dog Can Teach You 🐝 I just read about a dog named

Gidget in Glendale, California, who helps her master out on his job as parking lot attendant by dashing up to customers and collecting their validated tickets.

Her only reward, says her owner, is a pat on the head. This—as any good dog trainer will tell you—is as it should be.

Gidget's master has a good thing going for him, and I strongly suspect my uneasiness at reading the article is based on pure jealousy.

My dog, you see, is a 200 pound slob. He's never had a job and doesn't show any signs of going out to look for one. He does bring in the morning paper, but instead of dropping it obediently at my feet, he holds onto it.

He wants his cookie, and how much he wants his cookie I found out one morning when I discovered I'd run out of them.

"No cookie today," I said matter-of-factly to his black hulk, and gave him one of those supposedly valuable pats on the head. He sank his fangs more deeply into the headlines and sat down.

I gave him a bonus pat. He looked at me coldly and sighed. He had an air of insolent boredom about him—like a small-time hood waiting for protection money from a candy store owner. Frantically I searched the cupboards for a hard biscuit to satisfy him; he was beginning to drool through to the women's pages.

Hell, I thought, let him eat cake, and I cut him a wedge of German chocolate. He dropped the paper. I'll admit it: he has the upper paw.

I wasn't going to mention it, but Gidget collects those parking tickets wearing a pair of sunglasses and a little feathered hat. If it weren't so cute, it would make me sick. It's as bad as the kid next door who does his chores cheerfully, plays an instrument well, excels at sports, gets good grades, and is perfectly adjusted. I mean, I know dogs and kids like that exist, but I'd rather not think about them right now.

I'd like to take the dog on a walk and forget the whole thing, but I can't. He ate the leash.

Is Monday All Washed Up? 🦋 Monday is the ugly duckling of the week.

Poor little Monday. Why hasn't somebody declared it a national holiday instead of a national tragedy? "Ugh!" people say. "It's Monday."

Even dishtowels have things like, "Mondays we wash" embroidered thereon. Who says so? Why not, "Mondays we do as we please"?

Is Monday any shorter or any longer than any other day? Does the sun come up in black and white instead of color? Does it set with a plunk instead of the usual lovely slippage into the sea?

No. It's just that we have to gather ourselves together after a Sunday which, unfortunately, isn't all that Sunday used to be. Sunday is getting to be so full of jammed-to-getherness, and shopping at stores which remain open on that once cloistered day, that whether we like it or not, Monday has become a day of recuperation.

"Rest and Recuperation," I think the Army calls it, after a Sunday of stress. Just ask the employer. A lot of his employees have declared it a furlough–if not turning up at work is any indication. Or maybe AWOL would be more accurate.

Nevertheless, Monday, that innocent victim of our own foolishness and overindulgence, has suffered. Who ever heard of having a dinner party on Monday night? Or a cocktail party? A Monday night cocktail party would be so avant-garde, I'm surprised somebody hasn't already thought of it.

You know–let's do something really wild and kinky–like celebrating Monday. I don't know if Monday could stand it. After being used for washdays all these years, after being the medicinal 24 hours for turning hangovers into hang-in-theres, I really don't know if Monday could take the glare of such sudden affection.

It would be rather like handing an old maid a wedding bouquet on her eighty-first birthday. But for our own sakes, I think we ought to try.

Monday is a perfectly legitimate day, with all its minutes in good working order. To abandon it, if we live our predicted seventy-five years, is to hand over 4,400 days to nothingness.

I think that comes out roughly twelve years. That's a nice chunk of living, even if it is Monday.

Discounting the Years 🦋 We went to the

movies the other night, my husband and I, and we noticed there's a new age-price category. You now get in for a dollar less at some theaters if you'll admit to being over fifty-five.

Golden Age, it's called on the box office price list. And it isn't printed above the adult listing or even between adult and student, but at that humiliating position known as last, bottom or lowest. Even children, who pay the least amount, enjoy a better billing than the Golden Agers.

The couple in front of us looked as if they might

qualify, and the girl in the box office asked if they wanted Golden Age tickets.

The man, who probably conned his way into movies as a kid long after he was twelve to save a quarter, was now conning his way past the box office to pay a dollar more.

"Not me!" he said, glancing about himself nervously, "Maybe my wife here, ha, ha, ha, but not me."

His wife looked pained and smiled grimly. "Me neither," she said, and they passed for adults.

"What do you think?" I asked my husband. "Want to say we're fifty-five and save two dollars?"

He gave me his George Washington look. "That would be lying," he said.

"Yeah," I answered, "but we could bend over and wheeze a little. Two dollars is two dollars."

He sucked in his stomach and told me we'd never get away with it. And he was probably right. I mean, I'm not getting older–I'm just getting better–and he's still grabbing for all the gusto he can get.

But what's going to happen when we can't pass as adults anymore? Maybe it would help, even with the price of gold what it is today, if theaters called people over fifty-five Wisdom Agers instead of Golden Agers. And gave them a billing above adults so that along with slipping dentures and waistlines, they don't have to handle slipping prestige as well.

After all, eastern cultures have always elevated the aged and afforded them honor and respect. I'll never like egg foo yung, but when I get to be fifty-five, I think I'd rather go to the movies on the Ginza.

Don't Waste the Trash 🐝 Authorities

agree that children should have responsibilities around the house. Beginning at an early age, every kid worthy of the name should have his little area of endeavor.

Speaking as an overworked mother, I couldn't agree more. I'm all for anything that will lighten the load. But the problem is, those authorities suggest chores for kids that end up being more trouble than they're worth.

Take emptying the trash. That's a big favorite with child psychologists. It's their idea of a contribution to family living that will not only help mother but give the kid a sense of fulfillment.

I can't argue with the fulfillment angle, but as for helping mother–let me tell you: it all depends on what you have in your trash. Frankly, I'd rather quietly rush the wastebasket out to the trash barrels myself than fool around with my nine-year-old's efforts to get it there.

"Mom," he exclaims, "you aren't gonna throw out this swell bottle, are you?" There's something about an empty vodka bottle–it rises to the top of the wastebasket and catches the eye.

"Well, yes," I reply, "I was going to get rid of it, since it is used up." I try to treat it in much the same manner I would a bottle of Vaseline.

But it is my burden to have a creative son. "I'm going to take it to school and wrap it with yarn for my art project!" he says as he retrieves it enthusiastically.

"Now wait just a minute," I say, snatching it from him. "Your teacher would much rather have a smaller bottle– don't you think?"

But he is adamant. The vodka bottle or nothing. I can't think of a better way to get the PTA off my back, but somehow I can't bring myself to do it. At least not without some sort of explanation. So I write a note and slip it into the bottle.

"Dear Miss Watkins," it reads. "This bottle was emptied by my boy's father over a twelve-year period. Since it has been around the house so long, it is very dear to him and he wishes to preserve it in an art form with yarn and shellac. Your friend, Ann Rudy."

I may hear from Miss Watkins when it comes to making three dozen Christmas cookies, but I'll never make block mother. I just wish I'd never started that nonsense about helping around the house. If you really want to help me, kid, stay away from those wastebaskets.

Knock, Knock, Who's There? 🍎

Getting a kid to use the back door is an area of child training largely ignored by the experts. It is also an area of training largely ignored by the child.

For twelve years I have been cautioning my kids to "use the back door" in tones that can only be compared with a bull elephant's mating call. The elephant may get results, but I rarely do.

Oh, a couple of times I've gotten through to them and they've remembered to go the back way–all I have to do is wax the kitchen floor and they remember.

"Hey, it's slippery in here," said my eight-year-old the other day as he skated across the wet floor, followed by the neighborhood throng.

Don't say I'm not firm enough. I've told them both, again, and again, what I will do to them if they use that front door one more time.

Last week I told them. "Ring that front doorbell or walk in carrying a sandy towel, and I won't be responsible for my actions." I thought a veiled threat might do the trick, but it didn't. Five minutes after they left the house the front doorbell rang, and I mean to tell you I let them have it all the way down the hall on my way to answer it. By the time I had my hand on the knob to open it, I was bull-moosing it again. "You wanna drive me nuts?" I bellowed. "Quit ringing that bell before I belt you in the . . ."

Imagine my surprise when I swung open the door and found our parish priest standing there ready to make his yearly visit.

"Oh, hello, Father," I said, dropping a little curtsy, but it was too late. He had backed off down the walk.

"Just playing a little game with my kids," I called, but he was already in his car. For six months after that incident I answered the front door with a saccharine smile on my face and a cheery, "Hi, there!"

The bell rang 1,675 times and it was my kids 1,502 times. I did more performances than Mary Martin in *South Pacific*.

But I'm back to my old self now. "Stop running in and out of that front door or you'll really get it," I yelled just this morning.

Nobody paid any attention to me, and my discipline isn't any more effective than it ever was, but at least it's the real me.

Beware the Cordial Boy 🐛 You've heard

of overkill. But have you heard of overkind?

It's what happens to a kid when he tries to get his own way without using his usual methods. His usual methods include sulking, open combat, and arguments that make the Paris peace talks look like a convention of Quakers.

But with overkind, his whole approach is different–he becomes accommodating, genial, and generally too good to be true.

Only last week, after I had told my son he couldn't have an Irish setter because he already had a Newfoundland and another dog of unknown origins, he fell into overkind.

When his sister began to clear the table after dinner, he sprang from his chair and said "Let me, sis." This to a girl who has learned to duck when he raises his hand to comb his hair.

I found him sweeping out the garage with a smile on his face. He turned his radio off. He stopped belching. "OK," I said, "let's have it. What's on your mind?"

"Nothing," he answered, bringing me a chair so I wouldn't have to stand while undergoing the strain of talking to him. "It's just that . . . well, mom . . . a boy needs a dog."

When I reminded him that he already had two dogs who–though thoroughly delightful animals–did pose a problem at the door to incoming guests and salesmen who did not like to be aggressively licked by canines large enough to drive a bus. No matter. He was into overkind beyond recall.

"That's just it, mother," he said, "I want the dog for your sake."

I leaned forward in my chair, looked deep into his shifting eyes and said, "How's that again?"

"For your sake," he repeated. "An Irish setter would quiet the other two by diverting them, and then you wouldn't have to bother trying to call them off all the time with dog biscuits and pieces of raw meat."

I thought about it for a minute while he went off to fix me a pot of tea. When he returned he pulled up a chair to sit beside me and gave me a benign smile.

"I've decided," I told him. "The answer is still no. And it always will be. Now knock it off, buster, and get back to your old self."

No kidding, I liked him better when he belched.

The Bride:
Going, Going, Gone 🐞 I was surprised to
read that the price of brides in New Guinea has gone up.

And that the man in charge of trying to lower and stabilize prices is none other than Toua Kapena—the very fellow whose teen-age daughter just brought the record-breaking price of $6,700.

Come on, Toua, you can do better than that. If you're going to clamp down, start at home.

I mean, what are you going to do with those 34 bunches of bananas and 5 pigs? Not to mention the 56 bags of sugar and 1,010 seashells.

Isn't it enough that your future son-in-law had to put the bite on eleven relatives for loans to help him meet the cash down payment of $3,700? Those kids are just starting out and could use a few bananas themselves.

Loosen up, pop—you don't know how lucky you are. In this country, fathers pay to get rid of daughters. Only we call it a wedding. We have a tradition called "Giving the bride away," and that's just what it is.

Nobody collects except the groom, the caterer, the florist, the bridal shop and the distillery. After the reception the bride and groom drive off and leave dad standing in the driveway holding the bag—of rice. And he is supposed to throw even that after the departing couple.

Count your blessings, Toua.

If you have four or five more daughters still at home you've got it made. Even if you do have to come down a few pigs.

Just keep playing that old shell game of yours with the eligible young bachelors of New Guinea and you stand to make a fortune off the high cost of loving.

At Home with a Sore Ecology 🐛 If

I wanted to raise a fuss about environmental conditions, I could blow the lid off the whole ecology scene. And I could do it without leaving my house.

Talk about detergents in your drinking water—you don't know what pollution is until you find golf balls in the bottom of your tumblers. It's too much to swallow, and I told my family as much.

"But, mom," protested my son, who is learning to golf, "I have to practice my putting."

Then there is the oil slick problem. When a nine-year-old boy decides to make himself a bowl of popcorn while you are next door having coffee, you have an oil slick problem when you get home. He not only put oil in the popper; he anointed the floor, the sink, and six dishcloths with which he tried unsuccessfully to rectify the problem.

"Guess what, mom," he said as I came in the back door, "I made popcorn."

"No kidding," I said dryly, but my brilliant sarcasm was lost on him. Mainly because he couldn't hear me. He was literally up to his ears in popcorn—which proves it is not always the wisest thing to buy the giant economy size of anything.

As for the wildlife situation, I don't know what we are doing at our house, but it must be right, because the weevils, silverfish and ants don't show the slightest signs of future extinction.

I have so many weevils in my flour that my white sauce looks as though it has been seasoned with rye. Still, the beat goes on, and the insect birthrate at our house continues to boom. Makes you feel warm all over to know that somewhere in your cupboards lives a multitude of small crawling things who would not otherwise be there if not for you.

But it also makes you wonder if you might be contributing to the overpopulation crisis. The whole thing is very confusing.

I can only hope that we will all somehow survive, in our fashion, and I'll continue to cling to my guiding principle: Lips that touch DDT shall never touch mine.

Take My Dog–Please! 🦋 The popular

myth that a boy and his dog are inseparable has been exploded by our dog Higgins.

For the sake of kids everywhere, I only hope Higgins is the oddball we believe him to be. I'd hate to think there are boys scratching the ears of mutts from California to Connecticut who would just as soon the kid knocked it off.

For Higgins has the independence of a cat and is maddeningly aloof. He never spends the night in our boy's room unless the kid captures him.

I hadn't thought of Frank Buck for years until I saw the elaborate snare our son laid in the hallway. There was a trail of dog biscuits leading into a down quilt spread invitingly on the threshold of his room. All four corners of the quilt were tied with ropes, so that once Higgins began consuming the biscuits, step by step, he would walk into the quilt and nocturnal oblivion.

"Why don't you just let the dog sleep where he wants?" I asked.

"Because," the boy explained, "I like him and I want him to be by my bed."

Higgins, who by this time was in the folds of the quilt, gave me a look of sophisticated boredom. I showed the dog a Norman Rockwell print I had depicting boy-dog devotion. OK, I thought, if you're so blasé, take a look at what other dogs are up to. Stay in touch.

Higgins sniffed the picture and rolled tired eyes toward my son. His look seemed to say: "All right, I'll spend the night with you–but it's nothing permanent."

A truly contemporary dog. But his attitude is making inroads on our boy's psyche.

It's no fun to own a dog who makes you roll over before he will let you pat him. It's crushing if he barks and charges when you come in the front door. Especially after five years.

"If I were you," I advised my son, "I'd let sleeping dogs lie–in the living room."

He's thinking it over, and in the meantime I hope a really friendly down-home dog follows him home.

Danger: Exploding Myth 🐝 Who would

ever think a bathroom with a double basin could explode a common myth? For weeks I marveled at how clean my son's basin was, and shuddered at the sight of my daughter's. Hers was surrounded by brushes, combs, lotion bottles and other aids to feminine beauty, while the boy's basin was shiny-bright and his hand towel neatly folded on the rack. No wonder landladies would rather rent to young men, I thought. They certainly are neater–even as boys.

"Look how clean your brother's side of the bathroom is," I said to my daughter. "Why can't you pick up some of your rubble?"

I'll have to hand it to her: she kept quiet, although she must have known the truth. It was only after I noticed the same piece of pizza stuck to my boy's chin for three days that I too began to suspect the truth.

I ran downstairs and checked his bar of soap. It had been there two weeks and I could still read the lettering on it. I felt his toothbrush: dry. His washcloth still had the price tag on it.

I charged upstairs and pointed a trembling finger at him.

"You haven't been washing!" I accused.

"Aw, ma," he said sheepishly, dropping his eyes and plucking the pizza from his chin.

"You get down there and mess that bathroom up," I ordered. "Why can't you be as sloppy as your sister?"

He hadn't been in the bathroom for so long I had to show him where it was.

So, landladies and mothers of small boys, beware. Those clean basins and neat towels don't necessarily mean a fastidious fellow.

Maybe just a guy who knows how to comb his hair with his fingers, who hangs his clothes on a hickory limb and never goes near the water.

Walking Talking Pneumonia 🦠

Although medical men have been pondering a cure for the common cold for many years, it doesn't look as if they are going to come up with anything within the next few weeks.

That is really too bad, because the next few weeks, according to those who keep track of such things, are the peak of the cold season. If you happen to be a kid, it means you will get out of going to school for a few days and be able to watch *Divorce Court* on TV in the afternoons. But if you happen to be the kid's mother, it means you will probably catch it from him.

And what do you get out of? Nothing except a warm bed every morning to fix breakfast, pack lunches and quiz the kids on their spelling and the state capitals. Hardly what the doctor would order for a woman on the verge of bronchial pneumonia.

You should be flat on your back with a cough drop under your tongue. And you know it. You had every intention of going back to bed, but the seven-year-old forgot his lunch. If you don't get dressed and drive it to school, he will come home at noon.

Weakly you dress and deliver the banana and a bologna sandwich, stopping along the way to pick up the cleaning and buy four bags of groceries. Your life is hanging by a thread by the time you stagger into your bedroom two hours later.

You barely have the strength to turn down the bed, but you should have used it to tear the phone off the wall. It rings, and foolishly you answer it.

It is the PTA telling you there is no rush on the cookies you promised two weeks ago to bake–you can drop them off anytime within the next two hours.

Doggedly you dress again and head for the bakery. Buying bakery cookies that look homemade takes skill. You select three dozen irregular oatmeals which resemble what you might have made, had you not forgotten.

You drop them off at the meeting and spend an hour explaining why you can't stay. Three women take up another half hour telling you to go home and take care of yourself.

You arrive home just as school lets out. You get back into the car and drive daughter to dancing and son to drum lessons. After that, all you have to do is make dinner, do the dishes and fall into bed.

Oxygen tents, anyone?

Taking the Shirt Off Baby's Back 🦋 I heard a mother say, "Raise your arms" the other day while she was dressing her two-year-old and I thought: how quickly we forget key phrases that once made life so much easier.

Raise your arms, I haven't thought of that in years. Anybody who has ever dressed a baby knows what a milestone it is when the kid can finally cooperate.

The first time I tried to get a shirt off my infant daughter when I wasn't too much older than she was, I had to phone the doctor for help. The nurse had dressed her to go home from the hospital, and when we un-wrapped her, my husband and I, we realized it was up to us to get all those darling little clothes off.

He left the room; it was World Series time, and he made a man's choice.

I did pretty well until I got down to that shirt, and then anxiety set in. It was the kind that went over her head, and I had twelve more just like it. The nurse must have cheated, I thought. This baby's head is the size of a grapefruit and it simply won't go through that walnut-size opening.

Maybe I should leave it on until she outgrows it and then just cut it off. No, I hadn't read anything like that in my nine months of prenatal cramming.

First get the arms out, I remembered–calm yourself and get the arms out. But babies only have one elbow, and to get an arm out requires bending that tiny extremity in four places.

I put baby oil on her arms and tried to slide her out. I told her to inhale.

I rolled the shirt up around her neck, and, as I strug-gled, that perfect baby did an awesome thing: she began to cry. "Call the doctor!" I shouted to my husband. "She's stuck in her shirt!" But from the other room came only the sound of baseball and team spirit.

Clearly I was on my own. I picked her up and inched my way toward the phone. I couldn't decide between the fire department and the doctor but, anticipating surgery, I called the doctor. He was very kind. "Babies are tough," he said. "Go right ahead and wrestle with her."

So I went back and won two out of three falls. It only took eighteen more months of half nelsons and hammer-lock holds before she was finally able to understand those three wonderful little words: "Raise your arms."

After that it was clear sailing. Well, almost.

Christmas Cookies
I Have Blown 🐝 My Christmas cookies are a

tradition. The children wait for them—but they're not
allowed to throw them in the house.

My Christmas cookies are so bad the dogs in my
neighborhood won't turn over my garbage can during
December for fear of finding one. But I try; Betty Crocker
knows I try.

The trouble is, I do very well during the year with my
plain old lumpy oatmeal drop cookies, but at Christmas
time I see magazine articles about gay holiday cooking.
And there are always new cookie recipes that make me
think, "This time it will be different."

Full-color pictures of Yuletide tables set with plateloads
of Swedish, Hungarian and American cookie delights
work me up into such a pitch that before I can remember
the pfeffernuesse cookies I baked last year and gave out
as paperweights, I'm down at the market with a list of
ingredients.

And some of that stuff is not easy to find, let alone
pronounce. Let alone pay for. I mean, when a spice like
saffron comes all the way from Asia and requires 4,000
flowers to make one ounce, it costs so much it's a shame
to put it in your cookies. It belongs on your coffee table
along with the pre-Colombian god of fertility.

But I've put it in my cookies, along with everything else
I've been instructed to by those maddeningly efficient
home economists who are responsible for those magazine
layouts. But my Christmas cookies just don't come off. Off
my hands, off my rolling pin, off my teeth, and sometimes not even off the cookie sheet.

It's hard to be merry when you've had to scrape your
cookies off with a shovel while holding the baking sheet
down with one foot. But if the Christmas cookie crumbles,
fret not, for 'tis, after all, the season to be jolly.

Continental
Calorie Counting 🐛 Last Christmas a friend

gave me a copy of *The Low Calorie French Cookbook* by
Behoteguy de Teramond.

That's the kind of present you don't begin to think
about until the middle of April, and then you say to
yourself, "I needed that." In my case, I got the answer
when I tried to fasten last year's bathing suit and discovered I filled it not only out but up and over as well.

So I got the book out–and it works! I read to page 12
and began to lose my appetite. By page 45 I'd made up
my mind I'd rather starve than eat what Mrs. de Teramond had in mind.

How'd you like to sit down to a big plate of brains au
gratin with a little marinated kidney on the side? Or a jam
omelette topped off with apples stuffed with–brace yourself–onions?

The dust jacket says the author decided to write the
book after visiting this country and putting on 60 pounds.
On her return to France, she concocted the recipes, wrote
the book and dropped the 60 pounds.

I believe it. I've already lost three pounds running
around trying to find what the less revolting dishes call
for.

Try asking your butcher for a veal head. Where do I go
to get Armagnac–and can I bring my kids in there? For
fennel miraflores I'll need a small bunch of fennel and a
Gypsy to get it for me–along with the left foot of an
elderly owl.

But by far the biggest problem is what to tell my friend
who keeps asking, "How's the book–have you lost any
weight?"

Since the book weighs 24 ounces, I think I'll leave it on
a park bench–that way I can honestly tell her I've lost a
pound and a half.

How's that for thinking thin? *C'est magnifique!*

Stop, Ballerina, Stop! 🐛 The thing to re-

member about your little girl's taking ballet lessons is that
she probably will not become the premiere danseuse of
the Ballet Russe.

But if she keeps on playing that infernal practice record
and pirouetting endlessly around the dining table,
something else might happen. Something really dramatic–
like your mind snapping in the middle of dinner.

"Turn off that record," you will snarl, jumping onto
your chair in a half-crouch. "I can't stand it any longer!"

Depending on how often you flare up like this, your
family may do one of two things: throw cold water on
you, or go right on with their meal. But I guarantee you
one thing: your little girl will go on twirling.

That's how it is with ballet lessons; they get a girl
started and she just can't seem to stop. It's marvelous
training, of course, for later on when she marries and will
be required to repeat, again and again, such endless tasks
as washing, ironing and nose-wiping.

Her early training in ballet will enable her to bring a
kind of grace and fluid aplomb to her chores that will not
only impress her husband but bring many hours of visual
delight to the dog–or the parakeet, as the case may be.

As for her children, they will be able to take pride in
the fact that their mother is the only driver in the school
car pool who signals for a right turn with such a delicate
flick of the wrist.

Of course she may turn left after she does it, but few
kids have a mother who is both talented and a good
driver. So keep on providing your little girl with those
dance lessons and try to hold onto your sanity while she
practices at home.

And tell her father that in only a few short years he will
never again have to sit through a three-hour recital to see
thirty seconds of his own daughter.

Good Clean Family Art 🐝 We had an

explosion at our house the other day. It was a culture explosion.

We were all sitting around after dinner watching TV when it hit. Right in the middle of *The Gong Show* my husband said, "I bought a Picasso today." You could have knocked me over with a paintbrush.

"A Picasso?" I echoed, so taken aback that I spilled half my popcorn.

"That's right," he said. "Only $1.98."

At that price you might think it one of the artist's lesser works, but my husband assured me of the picture's worth. He said it had three nudes and a horse in it. The minute he mentioned nudes, the kids stopped watching *The Gong Show*. I put my popcorn aside as he described it more fully.

"What it is, really, is three sort of nude people getting a drink of water."

"Yeah?" said the twelve-year-old, and I quickly handed him the bowl of popcorn.

"What do you mean, 'sort-of nude'?" I snapped, jumping up from my chair. "That's like being sort of dead. If I'm going to put it in my living room, I want to know what those people have on–if anything."

"Now wait a minute," said my husband in a Vincent Price tone. "You know Picasso–everything is very vague–impressionistic."

I could see he'd been reading on his lunch hour, but I didn't let it throw me.

"Of course I know Picasso," I lied. "He's the one who cut off his ear."

"That was van Gogh," said the eight-year-old.

"You keep out of it," I cautioned. "Watch *The Gong Show.*"

But it was too late. Nobody was watching TV. My

husand was carrying on a monologue about Gauguin, Matisse, cubism, pointillism, and the importance of art in the home.

The twelve-year-old was all worked up and wanted to know if the Picasso was out in the car. And it was. It was in the glove compartment. For $1.98, that's about the size of it.

We brought it in and hung it next to the light switch for balance. Actually, I can't tell if those people are nude or not, but even if they are–I'll have to admit the picture has something to it. It's compelling.

And, whoever he is, I wish that fellow Picasso luck. I think he really has something going for him. But you know how people are about artists–he'll probably have to die before anybody appreciates him.

A Boy's Best Friend
Is His Mother 🐝 There is one thing that

turning forty does for you: it helps you to understand your mother-in-law.

For years I wondered why she couldn't stand me; now I am beginning to see why. It's not that I'm getting any wiser; it's that my son is getting older.

From the other side of my birthday cake, aflame with forty candles, I see my boy approaching puberty. Smoke gets in my eyes. Not that he's ready to get married or anything, but he no longer hates girls the way he used to. He doesn't really like them, either, but he has stopped throwing rocks at them, and last week he actually phoned a Camp Fire Girl who lives down the street.

That's when I thought of my mother-in-law. "What do you think of her, mom?" my son asked.

I replied, "She seems nice enough, but what does a

mother know? Girls today are hard to judge." Exactly what my mother-in-law said to my husband eighteen years ago.

She was so right. As it turned out, of course, I was a wonderful girl, but how was she to know? She isn't sure yet.

It's not that I expect any girl my son picks out to be perfect; it's only that I want her to be good enough for him. As long as she is pretty, comes from a good family, has high moral standards, maintains a 3.4 grade average and is well-groomed, healthy and willing to work to put him through his last two years of college, I couldn't care less about having any real say in the matter. Would any boy's mother?

Of course he's only eleven and has years to go yet before getting serious about one girl. As I said to him, that Camp Fire Girl is pretty wrapped up in wood carving right now and doesn't seem the type to take an interest in anything he likes.

Then I gave him two pieces of apple pie and pulled the phone off the wall. I think he understands, I really do.

In the words of that wonderful woman, my mother-in-law, I'm only thinking of his good. I don't want him to get stuck with just another pretty face who will give him nothing but the best years of her life, three fine children and forty years of love and companionship. Not if I can help it.

Monday Morning
Sick Calls 🐛 Having a child home sick in bed
helps a mother discover things about herself.

If you are curious about your breaking point, or even your boiling point, try playing Florence Nightingale to a

child with nothing more serious than a subclinical infection.

Subclinical infection is what the pediatrician calls a
minor, vague illness he can't identify.

I've done a little research on subclinical infections, and
I've found they usually strike on Monday mornings or just
before a test at school.

The symptoms may be anything from a sore throat to
stomach cramps, but they subside dramatically as soon as
the school bus pulls away from the curb–leaving you with
a patient who is probably in better shape than you are.

Propped up in his bed, surrounded by comic books and
oozing energy, he calls for breakfast.

Then he calls for the portable TV.

Then he just calls.

And calls.

For a kid with a sore throat, his larynx is in prime
condition. The last time this happened to me, I told my
boy not to keep calling unless it was an emergency. If
there was a boa constrictor in his room, I'd come in and
handle things–otherwise, don't call. Would you believe he
had thirty-seven emergencies before noon?

The only time he shut his mouth was when I tried to
give him his medicine.

And he needed that medicine, because anyone could
see he was in critical condition–he criticized everything:
his soup was too hot, his pillow was too soft, and there
were crumbs in his bed.

There was a dog, a white rat and a Scrabble game in his
bed too, but none of these seemed to bother him.

Not as much as they bothered me, anyway.

By the end of the day I wasn't feeling so good myself.
Not really sick, mind you; just sort of a subclinical
infection.

Bedroom Sonics 🦋 Whether you are under

the same covers with one or just under the same roof, a snorer can keep the whole house as wide-eyed as a dead fish.

My husband is a third-generation snorer but is very modest about his heritage. He denies he snores at all.

Just the other night I shoved him in the ribs with my elbow at 3 A.M. and said, "Turn over. You're at it again."

His response was immediate. He rolled over and said humbly, "I'm not even asleep." If he can make sounds like that when he's awake, I hope he never sleeps.

If I were in the mood to appreciate it, I'd think he was on to a new sound in snoring.

It isn't the usual inhaling and exhaling of postnasal sonics—it is full of paradiddles.

I might even get used to it if I were a student of way-out sounds, but as soon as he gets my attention, he stops. Not for long, of course, but just long enough to worry me. By the time I turn on the bedroom light and hold a mirror in front of his mouth to see if he is still breathing, he is off again—gargling marbles, fluttering his pharynx and snorting sporadically.

I'd swear he was asleep if I didn't know he was awake.

Other women whose husbands snore have suggested that I try holding his nose or turning the electric blanket up to very hot. They have all kinds of ideas.

So we have organized a National Association for the Prevention of Snoring: NAPS.

However, we have taken our men for better or for worse, inhaling or exhaling, until sound barriers they do break.

But if you happen to know of a sure-fire remedy for snoring, drop around to a NAPS meeting sometime and let us in on it.

Knock softly. We may be asleep.

The Problem Parent
from 25 to 50 🍎 Parents can turn to any

number of sources today when perplexed about their
children. Child psychologists. Authoritative books. For-
tune-tellers.

But what can a child do when parents are a problem?
There is virtually nothing written for kids about how to
handle a mother and father who are between the ages of
twenty-five and fifty.

The little dears have to go it completely on their own;
and let me tell you, by the time they hit twelve or
thirteen, they've just about had it with us and are ready
to do us irreparable psychic harm.

The other night as she was waiting for her guests to
arrive for a little get-together, my daughter asked carefully, "You and daddy aren't going to come in, are you?" I
knew just how she felt. We felt the same way about her
when she was three and we had a party. Only we read
Spock, and he told us how to handle it.

We let her come in, pass the canapés and sing one
verse of "There Was an Old Woman Who Swallowed a
Fly." (Spock should have written another chapter on how
to stop a kid after one verse.)

At any rate, how could my twelve-year-old know that
the best way to handle us would be to let us come in for
a minute or two, play our Glen Miller record and show
the kids how to truck on down?

Then we would have gone happily to our room. Instead, she told us not to hang around and keep peeking
through the living room door. It's painful to be rejected at
any age.

She has given me a shopping trauma too. While out
looking for a pair of jeans, I told her the ones she was
trying on were too small; I could tell because her navel

was showing. "Mother," she said, giving the salesgirl, who was pushing seventeen, a pained look, "navels are 'in.'"

Now I wouldn't buy her a toothbrush without checking with her first. And I suspect I'm a disappointment to our seven-year-old too. "Mom, when you were little," he asked yesterday as he studied my crow's feet in the morning light, "did you ever see a dinosaur?"

"No," I answered, "but I saw Benny Goodman at the 1939 World's Fair."

He was unimpressed.

Keeping an Old Flame New 🐝

Contrary to what most women believe, it is not their husbands who kill romance after marriage, it is themselves.

But don't feel badly, dears. Try what I tried last week when I realized with a pang that "our song"–"Smoke Gets in Your Eyes"–had become, over the years, "Ashes Get On Your Coffee Table." I sat down and had a head-to-head talk with my husband.

"Listen," I said to him, "there's nothing left to find out between us anymore, except, perhaps, how long can you keep up that infernal snoring?" (He was awake at the time, so even that mystery didn't count.)

"You mean you want it to be like before we were married?" he asked.

"Yeah," I answered, amazed that he could be so sensitive to my needs. "You know," I encouraged. "Remember how you used to keep me guessing? And buy me presents we couldn't afford?"

"Yes," he recalled. "And how you used to knit me argyle socks, laugh at my jokes and bake me those four-layer cakes that took all day?" He was so excited he dropped the sports page he was reading and jumped up from his chair.

"And remember," he continued, advancing upon me, "how you used to make my sport shirts? And wait up for me no matter how late I worked, with those great sandwiches–and the garnish that only you could think of?"

I sat down slowly on the hassock and said, "Now wait just a minute. You certainly don't expect a return to that sort of thing, do you? I mean, I'll make you a sandwich if you want, but you'll have to remember that my garnish isn't what it used to be."

That seemed to satisfy him. He returned to the sports page and only looked up when I asked him if he had remembered to paint the interior of the shower which had lately showed signs of growing moss.

"Maybe I did, and maybe I didn't," he said, glancing at me rakishly, and added, "How's that for keeping you guessing?"

"Stop it, you fool," I answered. "First thing you know you'll have me making you a sandwich."

Santa Baby, Say No 🐝 If my Christmas

warning seems a little early, it is because I wish someone had cautioned me in time last year–and the year before.

Mothers and fathers of small sons, beware. Now is the time little boys begin to tell you that they want two classic things for Christmas.

The first is a microscope. When my son asked for one two years ago, I took time out from scraping carrots at the sink and sat down to take a better look at him.

Why hadn't I seen it before? The delicate cut of his nose–so like Louis Pasteur. The low ears and high forehead my mother always said indicated brilliance. My boy with a microscope. Bending over it late into the night, winning first place at the school science fair.

So we got our seven-year-old a microscope with a high-powered zoom lens and enough slides to keep him occupied until his scholarship from Johns Hopkins came through.

But it didn't turn out quite that way. He found he enjoyed the slides more if he used their sharp edges to scrape the varnish off his bedroom furniture.

As for the microscope, he's sorry, but what he really wanted was something that would permit him to see through flesh and bones. Like an X-ray machine.

You can't win 'em all—but we tried the next year when we got him the drums he asked for. That's the other classic request which parents would do best to ignore. It's not the noise, because after the first few awful weeks our boy never played them.

But where do you keep a full set of drums, complete with cymbal? Right in the middle of the floor, that's where—all year.

The last time I vacuumed around them I fell over the cord and did two choruses of "Drum Boogie" before I got to my feet. So go slow if your boy asks for drum or a microscope this year.

Of course, if the kid is very unusual—talented and all that—I can let you have both items at practically wholesale.

Brace Yourself
for Dental Perfection 🍎 Along with every-

thing else, the cost of straightening a child's teeth has climbed since the days when braces were called bands.

Today, giving a kid a nice smile costs so much it's the parents who end up unable to smile. By the time the child's teeth are right, there's nothing left. He has more silver in his mouth than you'll ever have in your pocket.

You could have gone to Europe twice on what it will cost you to bring his teeth to heel. But it's worth it. The day will come when he will thank you.

The day will come, but don't hold your breath. Right now, he hates you for sending him to the orthodontist. He hates the orthodontist, too. Both of you are responsible for the fact that he now has a smile like the rear end of a Thunderbird.

If he could have either one of you rubbed out, it would be a toss-up. Any child who is forced to wear a headgear twelves hours a day is looking for a good triggerman.

He also is looking for something to eat. The dentist has warned him against candy, gum, dried fruit, corn on the cob, and anything else that requires hard biting or chewing. Eat anything on the forbidden list and the work the orthodontist did with his soldering iron may be undone— but the child will not get a toothache.

He will not get a toothache because his braces are screwed so tight he already has one. In fact, he has thirty-two aches. His mouth is so sore he can hardly open it to tell you how miserable you've made him.

But children are resilient creatures, and they find ways to compensate. With practice, a kid can learn to open his mouth in such a way that the rubber bands fly off the braces and zing clear across the room. Granted, this is no way for a child to say thank you, but it will have to do until the braces are removed and he can smile at you and mean it.

Year of the Bore 🐛 My husband tells me this

is the Chinese year of the bore. Or maybe it was boar.

But since he isn't Chinese and since he didn't spell it

for me, I am taking a closer look at myself. I mean, maybe he was trying to tell me something.

Have I really been holding up my end of our conversations lately? Just yesterday he sat down across from me and launched into a subject I didn't feel I could discuss adequately. It concerned our heating system.

"Have you noticed," he began, "that funny ticking sound when the furnace first goes on?"

I could only look at him blankly. How could I explain that for survival's sake I have learned to tune out all sounds save shouts of fire and rape?

Otherwise, I would long ago have been impaled on the antennas of transistor radios, clobbered into senselessness by the patter of tiny feet, and flattened by the incessant shouts for just one more glass of water. The day I hear the furnace ticking may well be the day I hear my own teeth decaying or the termites at work in the basement.

Finally I said, "What ticking?" which of course was no help at all, and certainly far from a stimulating answer.

But my husband is relentless, so he tried another tack. "Forget the furnace," he said. "Where is the key to that trunk out in the garage?"

I didn't even know we had a trunk out in the garage. So I told him not to worry about unlocking the trunk–that if there was anything worth having in it I would have the key on a string around my neck.

"You don't have the key," he said flatly, and I sprang from my chair in an effort not to disappoint him.

"Oh, yes, I do have some keys. Wait here."

I was back in a few minutes with a shoe box full of keys. I don't know how many I've collected, but the box weighs about 25 pounds.

"It's probably in here," I said, and picked out a brass key that was turning green.

"Is this it?"

He just looked at me, and I sensed that my chance for

116

meaningful verbal exchange had passed. No wonder he falls asleep after dinner.

What can I say, except Happy Chinese New Year?

Granny, Tell Me More 🐝 I don't know

what Helen Gurley Brown would think of my grandmother, but I'm sure my grandmother would have an opinion about Helen Gurley Brown. My grandmother had an opinion about everything and everybody.

Her opinions weren't always right, but they were always definite. If she made a mistake, she made it with conviction.

Helen Gurley Brown would find no shrinking Victorian violet lurking behind grandma's summary of a former suitor: "He wasn't worth the powder and lead to blow him uphill."

"Really, grandma?" I would say, drawing my chair closer in case there was more to come.

And there always was. "No, sirree! he was a chair-presser."

To grandma, there was nothing worse than a chair-presser—a boy who came to call and remained sitting in the girl's living room all evening without offering to walk her to the corner ice cream parlor.

Chair-pressers never presented a box of candy when they called, and they always ate the top layer from a box somebody else had brought.

Hopeless cases pulled open the little side drawers of the box and helped themselves to the fancy foil-wrapped pieces.

To grandma, behavior like this was unforgivable. She never had any trouble making up her mind about a chair-presser. "I wouldn't have had him if every hair on his head was strung with a diamond." This always seemed a little hasty to me–picturing every hair on some-body's head strung with a diamond–but grandma had nine proposals, so she must have known what she was doing.

"What did you do when you wanted to get rid of a boy, grandma?" I used to ask, enthralled. Grandma would lean forward in her chair, give me a wink and say brightly, "Why, I'd simply give him his walking papers."

I have no doubt that she did–without any help from Helen Gurley Brown. And when I consider that grandma was doing this in 1906, I can't help viewing Helen Gurley Brown's efforts to free the American woman from her Victorian shackles with a twinkle in my eye. Grandma could have told her a thing or two.

Hole-Digging Revisited 🦋 Now that

school is out, some of you may be wondering what to do with your children. Some of you may even be wondering why you ever had children; but if you will stop and think for a moment, you will have some answers.

There are several things kids used to do that have passed out of fashion and need only new packaging to bring excitement into tiny lives. Hole-digging, for instance. You don't tell your child to go dig a hole because that is a drag. It's been years since Robert Louis Stevenson dug a hole beside the sea and got a kick out of it.

Today you have to make it a real challenge. So you say to your ten-year-old boy: "I read in the paper that some teen-age boys have been digging holes. Isn't that awful?"

Your boy will say: "Heck, no. Why shouldn't they? They've got as much right as parents to dig holes."

Then you close in for the kill with: "I wouldn't be caught dead digging a hole. It is a complete waste of time, and furthermore, I don't want you to even mention digging a hole."

Within three days his desire for hole-digging will be at such a high pitch that he will offer to pay you for the use of daddy's shovel and the far northwest corner of the backyard. Once he gets going, a good hole can take days, and it is exhausting work. He will be too weak to argue about bedtime or fight with his sister when he finally comes into the house.

And what about the lost art of tree-sitting? The best way to get a boy to climb a tree is to come into his room first thing in the morning and tell him that today is the day you are going to help him clean it up.

But first you are taking him downtown for a haircut. He will be up the nearest tree before you can say, "Come back here." It will be the first time in months he has been without transistorized music, TV, and a gang of friends.

Up there he will notice the way young leaves are tender and transparent while the old ones are thick and opaque. By the time he comes down he will be a beginning philosopher.

Mother, Take a Bow 🐝 Casting directors
often look for months before they find the type they want, so if you know of one who is looking for a middle-aged heavy who makes a great peanut butter sandwich, send him around.

I'd also be good as a killjoy, wet blanket, and all-around spoil-sport.

I didn't realize I had so much talent until my kids told me. They are very alert and have a discerning eye. It was just after I had refused to give my thirteen-year-old a private phone that she first saw my possibilities.

"Gee, mom," she said, "you are a real drag."

The seven-year-old was quick to back up his sister. "Yeah," he said. "You never let us have any fun."

"I'm just like everybody else's mother," I said modestly; but they would have none of it.

"Oh no you aren't," they chorused. "You are the meanest mother in the whole world."

They have always wanted me to be first in everything, and I could never have done it without them.

The darling way my boy nags and nags about not being allowed to play on the railroad tracks. The cute little trick my daughter has of leaving her clothes all over the bathroom. The apple cores in the flower arrangements, the sugar on the kitchen floor—with this kind of support, how could I miss? They've been behind me all the way.

But it takes work. Just yesterday I saw how quickly I could slip if I wasn't careful. It had been a long day, and I was tired. They wanted to eat half an apple pie before dinner and I said yes.

"You're the greatest!" they said happily.

A few more mistakes like that and I could be all washed up.

Summertime, and the Learnin' Ain't Easy 🐝 Summer

school notices have been drifting home from school lately and are being received with mixed emotions. The seven-year-old's was rolled up in his back pocket along with an original crayon drawing of Batman and himself.

I rescued this valuable packet just before I tossed his jeans into the washing machine last week. "Oh, look what I found in your pocket," I marveled, as he was spooning in the last of his morning cereal.

"Yeah, I drew that picture of me and Batman."

"I meant the summer school notice," I answered. "You can go to school this summer if you want and have a lot of fun."

Surprised, he stopped his spoon in midair and asked, "Doing what?"

I realized that this was a loaded question and that my answer could push him in either direction. I remembered how the school cafeteria menu used adjectives to enhance the fare.

Applesauce was "rosy." Potatoes were "fluffy." "You will have exciting arithmetic, gay spelling and worthwhile reading," I said.

He made up his mind immediately. His "I'm not goin'" was definite. I think I made a mistake saying "worthwhile."

To lure children in the upper grades, the school has added something new this year. It is called Fine Arts Seminar and is described as "a new and exciting learning opportunity."

The twelve-year-old brought this information home and quietly laid it on the table, just the way she brings home vaccination permits.

She hoped I wouldn't notice, but of course I did. "Well," I said, "this is really something. Are you going to enjoy this! Field trips, creative productions, and special guest speakers! Fluffy whipped potatoes and rosy applesauce!"

She exchanged a long look with her brother. "Mother," she said, "you just want to get rid of us in the mornings this summer."

With insight like that it is a shame she won't be developing it further this summer, but it looks as if she won't. And I won't get to read the papers undisturbed in the morning this summer either.

Oh, well, if summer comes, can fall be far behind?

The Round-the-Clock Wonder Diet ❦ I don't have any trouble sticking to a diet, and I honestly can't see what people mean when they say it takes great willpower.

I've been dieting for three days now, and I've eaten everything I was supposed to. Every bite.

For breakfast the first day I had half a grapefruit, dry toast, black coffee and a boiled egg. Easy as that, and I didn't feel the least bit hungry afterwards–just proud of myself. Good for me, I thought. I got through the first meal with flying colors.

A kind of euphoria comes over the successful dieter, and you want to share your joy with everyone. So I went next door to tell my neighbor how simple it was. Over coffee and two doughnuts, I told her she should try it.

Lunch was just as easy–cottage cheese, half a tomato, tea and dry toast. So easy–and nourishing too.

I hardly had any appetite for the chocolate sundae the kids talked me into downtown, but if you pay for something you really ought to eat it.

Dinner is the same every night: a slice of cold chicken, clear soup, steamed broccoli and skim milk. I've stuck to it faithfully.

Of course I wouldn't feed the rest of my family the diet fare. They need fuel to keep going.

The dinner includes plenty of meat, potatoes, gravy, muffins with butter and honey–or something equally hearty. And they like dessert too.

I never eat dessert, because to tell you the truth, by the time I finish eating their leftovers, I really don't want lemon pie or anything like it.

Actually, I prefer a small glass of low-cal cranberry juice just before bed. That's allowed.

As I said to my husband the other night while we were

having pastrami sandwiches and malts after a movie, once you make up your mind to eat exactly what is printed on the diet menu, the rest just sort of comes naturally.

Are Newspapers Necessary? 🐝

Thoreau, in *Walden*, said he never read any memorable news in a newspaper. "News," he wrote, "is gossip, and those who edit and read it are old women over their tea." He never did get down to what is good about newspapers.

I think this is a great injustice and a direct slap in the face to the millions of people who couldn't get along without newspapers. Take schoolchildren. Every few months the schools have a paper drive which provides after school activity for hundreds of bored kids. Children take to the streets pulling wagons and ringing doorbells during the dinner hour, hoping to get your old newspapers. On a windy day, the circulation of these untied papers would surprise many an editor.

Certainly no one who ever trained a new puppy would underestimate the importance of a daily newspaper.

What washes windows cleaner? Starts a fire quicker?

Thoreau put so much emphasis on economy, I'm surprised he didn't realize that the sports page is cheaper and more effective than French perfume when it comes to luring a lazy husband to the breakfast table.

It is perfectly obvious that Thoreau never packed a china service for twenty-four when he moved to Concord, or he would have had more reverence for newspapers.

But even if you don't read them or use them, you can still enjoy newspapers, because they are nostalgic. Would Sunday be Sunday without a patchwork of funnies on the living room floor? Part of the happy picture of a father's evening return home always includes a paper under his arm. And the delivery boy is ageless: pedaling his bike with the bulging canvas bag over the handlebars–throwing papers and imagining with every toss it is a big league ball.

Like handshakes and hellos, like hot dogs and babies' kisses, who could imagine life without newspapers?

Is There a Rat in the House? 🐞 The

rat across the street had rats the other day, and the seven-year-old has announced breathlessly that we can have one if we want. And free.

This is the sort of windfall any seven-year-old in his right mind snaps up immediately and any mother in her right mind says no to immediately.

The white rat may be free, but unless you want to give him the run of the house, you have to buy him a $10 cage.

Nobody likes a flabby rat, so you had better throw in that four-dollar exercise wheel. Exercise makes rats thirsty, so include a 75-cent water bottle.

Then there's shavings for the cage floor, and rodent food, which brings the grand total to just thirty cents short of the seven-year-old's allowance for the next two years.

That's a long time to go without monster stickers, but he promises to live an ascetic life stripped of all childhood comforts.

He promises to care for the rat as if he were a rare orchid, to listen for his stirrings in the night, and to love him like a brother.

Then when daddy comes home and you both have had your martinis, you agree that if the seven-year-old will really do all he promises, a rat is just what you need.

So two weeks later the rodent is part of your household and the seven-year-old is back on his allowance. Nothing has really changed except that the rat is crazy about you because he knows you are the one with the food.

And you are the one who makes his shavings comfy. And you are the one with the water. If it weren't that you never wanted him in the first place, you might even find yourself liking him back a little.

But as it is, could anyone blame you for trying to build a better mousetrap?

Halloween Haute Couture 🦋 As Hal-

loween approaches, nervous mothers eye the rag pile wondering what is available for costume-making.

Since I am a veteran of many Halloweens, let me tell you it is all in the power of suggestion.

"How would you like to be a ghost?" you say in an upbeat manner. Your eight-year-old fixes you with a jaded eye and says firmly, "I want to be Zorro!" You may as well forget throwing that worn-out sheet over him. He wants to be Zorro. As for that power of suggestion bit, I meant his power, not yours. The kid is going to be whatever he wants to be, whether it is Zorro or Fidel Castro.

Your only problem will be where to dig up his costume. Forget about buying any of those ready-made getups of Bugs Bunny or Little Red Riding Hood. The store outfits are not three-dimensional—everything is stamped on, and unless your child is under two he will know the difference. Kids today want authenticity. Marie Antoinette with her head under her arm, Jack the Ripper with his switchblade open—that sort of thing.

As for me, all I care about is whether or not he is warm

as he goes from door to door in search of penny treats. If there is room under his costume for a pair of long pants and a sweater, Jack the Ripper can't be all bad.

It's the girls decked out as Isadora Duncan who worry me. After two hours of doorbell-ringing, they come home with twelve pounds of cheap candy and walking pneumonia.

But it's all in the name of childhood.

Pick Your Picnic Spot
with Care 🌴 There are more things to worry
about on a family picnic than ants. Actually, ants often prove a blessing, as they are an excuse for going home.

"Oh, look," I said to my husband just last Sunday, "there's a line of ants heading our way." Being very quick on the uptake, he said, "Good. Let's go home."

He had been sitting under a dead tree on a plastic dropcloth for a quarter of an hour while I unpacked the lunch on a table provided by the state, county, or some other faceless source. It had been painted green and was overlaid with a fine layer of dust and dried mustard.

Chained to one end of the table was a matching trashcan filled with indisputable evidence that others before us had found it possible to eat here. Twenty yards distant, the kids were milling around in new sneakers looking for the delights of nature I had promised them.

"I don't see any chipmunks," said the seven-year-old, turning over a stone with the toe of his shoe. "Well, you have to look," I snapped, not at all like a ranger. "What do you expect only a mile from the freeway? After all, this is just a little family picnic, not Yosemite."

The thirteen-year-old gave a wail of alarm. We all froze. But it wasn't a rattlesnake or even a chipmunk. She had forgotten her comb.

126

I hopefully dropped a few cake crumbs to encourage the ants. Pretty soon they were everywhere. Even the kids thought it was a good idea to go home.

But don't let me discourage you. Go ahead. Pack that lunch you want–and drive around until you find a nice, old-fashioned picnic ground where you can spread out under shade trees while your watermelon cools nearby in an icy stream.

Don't Toy with
My Lace-Edged Heart 🍑 There was a

time when valentines were exchanged only between people who liked each other especially well. You didn't have to be full-grown or anything. You could even be six with a couple of teeth missing in front. But you had to be a girl and he had to be a boy, and the whole thing became very exciting.

Maybe he carried the valentine around all day before he worked up enough nerve to give it to you; but when he finally did, grubby or not, it was the nicest piece of paper in the whole world.

You were somebody's valentine.

Things are more organized today. The teacher sends home a mimeographed list of the kids in class so Freddie will be sure to spell all thirty-two names correctly and not leave anybody out.

Valentines have become a chore. "Do I have to send Mike one?" asks Freddie, toying with a lace-edged heart. "He eats paste."

"I don't care what he does," answers mother. "You can't leave him out."

And so it goes. Even for grown-ups, it's an up-hill battle to keep things romantic.

I was only going to buy one valentine until I saw the display of cards professing undying love for such people as my secret pal, my mother-in-law, and a fine nephew.

These people are all simply grand, but I wouldn't want to hold hands in the movies with any of them.

Even the dairies are contributing to the confusion. Last week my milkman left a long pink card with red lettering. "Roses are red, violets are blue," it said; "for your being our customer, we really love you."

I'll have to admit this declaration caught me completely off guard, and my heart quickened beneath my quilted robe as I read on in the predawn light. ". . . and to prove it, we are offering you two dozen large AA eggs for only 99 cents."

No woman likes to be led on. I don't care how great a protein buy those eggs may be, let's keep it impersonal.

I did order the eggs; I needed them anyway. But my note in the milk bottle was very prim.

I'd hate for him to start carrying a torch along with all that yogurt and sour cream.

The Plumber's My Friend ❦ Next to

going into labor in a stalled elevator, the worst thing I can think of is having the plumbing back up on a Monday morning. I guess I should rejoice that only the second worst thing happened to me, but I don't know.

I've always wanted to go to Venice, only I never dreamed my center hall would be my Italy. As I paddled my way down that hall last Monday, toward the phone, I tried to think of reasons to be grateful. But it was no good.

"Look, girl," I said to myself, "your plumbing has backed up; it's as simple as that. Don't try to philosophize it into a glad event."

I like it when I level with myself that way. So instead of telling the plumber to drop by for a little Italian brunch and a spot of wine, I told him my Grand Canal needed attention immediately. That's as honest as I could be, considering my romantic nature.

"Okay, lady," he said, "I'll be right over with a snake."

I figured he had a hangup about Cleopatra on her barge because when you are in the sewer game you have to escape reality somehow. After all, if I thought I was in Venice, the least I could do was let him think I was Celopatra in need of an asp.

But when we set sail into that hall together, it was a moment of truth. "How many towels ya got on hand?" he asked; and I, taking inventory of the linen closet as we passed by, answered, "Not enough, buddy; not enough."

We looked into each other's eyes and knew complete frustration.

That's the way it is on Monday morning when the tide is against you.

But we solved it, the plumber and I; he with his professional skill, and I with an inordinate amount of sublimation. After he rendered my hallway dry, I stood in the front doorway and waved at his departing truck which had TONY'S PLUMBING SERVICE lettered on the side panel and whispered, "Good-bye, Antonio, good-bye."

Except for the twenty-seven soggy towels at my feet, I felt just like Katharine Hepburn in *Summertime*.

Scrooge Takes a Holiday 🍎 Scrooge

wasn't the first man to have second thoughts a few days before Christmas, nor will he be the last. Every year Scrooges may be detected here and there–maybe even in your own family.

Here are the signs:

Last October your husband told you that Christmas was a commercial holocaust and that he personally didn't intend to become involved; all he wanted was peace and quiet.

Two days before Christmas, he sees a foil-covered Santa in a candy store window and remembers the time–when he was seven–he found one just like it in the toe of his stocking–along with an orange and a walnut.

A foil-covered Santa, given in love so long ago, will rise out of a man's memory like a Christmas ghost to remind him of love given.

He goes into the candy store, and when he comes out, the tight little line beside his mouth has relaxed. And laying a finger aside of his nose, he gets out his credit card and into debt he goes.

Sometimes Scrooges are female. Maybe it's a mother who is tired of hearing her children repeat endlessly what they want. Unable to supply them with the new $50 bikes they desire, she decides Christmas has corrupted the young.

Then, a few days before Christmas, she finds, on the top shelf of her children's closet, two tiny packages they have wrapped with loving hands. Printed laboriously on one card is: "To Mom. I love you, even if I don't get the bike."

That woman is the woman you see, out at the last minute, buying what she can afford with the true Christmas light shining in her eyes. Because she knows, just as our friend Scrooge finally knew, that love is what Christmas is all about.

Whether you wrap it in fancy ribbons or give it out heart-to-heart, it is the only gift of any real value.

A Loaf of Bread, a Gallon of Paint, and Thou 🦋

There was a time when my husband and I thought it was a big treat to stay home all weekend and paint the living room.

Those were the lovely, tender years when the joy of having an extra $5 for a gallon of paint was superseded only by the elation of standing back and seeing all four walls newly coated in parchment beige.

Our apartment was so small we even had enough paint left over for the hall—and the bedroom. But things have changed.

After painting our way through seventeen years, four apartments and three houses, our enthusiasm isn't what it used to be.

This year we decided to have it done. After I called the painters, I pictured myself sitting on the sofa with a cup of coffee while somebody else crawled around painting the baseboards. It was a lovely and well-deserved dream.

But, like all dreams, it faded in the bright light of morning. In my case, reality knocked on the front door at 6:30. Clutching my quilted robe about me, I opened the door a crack and saw, to my horror, two bright-eyed painters standing there.

"Are you out of the kitchen yet?" they asked, stepping across the threshold with all the authority of the vice squad.

"Yes," I lied. The truth was, I hadn't even been in the kitchen yet.

They began work immediately, slapping paint on everything, while I scurried down the hall to warn everybody.

"Get up!" I hissed. "Get up! They're here."

"Who?" my husband asked sleepily.

"The painters!" screeched my eight-year-old son in wild jubilation. "And I'm gonna help 'em." Then he ran, half-nude, down the hall toward the kitchen. I fielded him with one arm and knocked on my daughter's door with my free hand.

"Hit the deck!" I called in growing hysteria. "You all have to be dressed and out of the kitchen in five minutes." It took them an hour and they never did get into the kitchen. They went off to work and school and left me there to enjoy the luxury of the painters.

One was a compulsive talker, and the other had an unquenchable thirst for coffee.

And even though they painted the ceilings, the baseboards and all those nerve-wracking windowsills with professional ease, I'll have to admit—nothing is quite so much fun as a $5 gallon of paint seventeen years ago.

Fashion Can Be Wearing 🦋 There's a

sort of cruel irony happening in the fashion world today, and I find I truly haven't a thing to wear. Oh, I know women have been saying that twice a year and every weekend for centuries, but this time I mean it.

The thing is, what has become the "latest" thing is something I remember wearing when I was younger. What's fresh to my daughter is warmed over to me, and she can't understand why I'm not more enthusiastic about a forties dress and a pair of Fred Astaire pants.

I've tried to tell her that the last time I wore a dress like that I was seventeen and had nothing more on my mind than how to keep last night's gardenia corsage from turning brown. Well, alas, my dear daughter, that gardenia is long gone, and so is my girlish figure.

There is as much harsh reality in trying on a dress like the one I wore to the senior hop in 1945 as there is in a twenty-fifth-year class reunion. Take all those balding middle-aged men away, I tell you; they are not the boys I used to know.

As for the Fred Astaire pants, Fred Astaire was a father figure to me. I would watch him and think, Gee, he's good–I don't care if he is forty-one. I'd like to continue to think of him as a father figure, except that he doesn't look any older today than he did then, and he hasn't put on an ounce. I'm the same age now as he was then, only now I'm too fat for his pants. Besides, I've forgotten all the words to "Top Hat."

If we are going to turn back the fashion clock, why can't we give it a really good twist to, say, 1900?

Then I could go shopping and return home with a new outfit and say to my husband, "Just look at this darling dress I found today. I remember seeing pictures of my grandmother in one just like it–pictures taken long before I was born, of course."

And he would look at me critically and say, "Return it. It's too old for you." I still wouldn't have a thing to wear, but I'd be walking on air.

I Like a Gershwin Tune; How About You? 🦋 "Mother," said my

daughter after her first college dance, "it was the best time I've ever had–they played all the old favorites."

At last, I thought, she has learned to two-step to "Star Dust." But I was wrong.

"Old favorites," she continued, "like 'Rock Around the Clock,' 'Let's Go to the Hop' and 'Twisting U.S.A.' "

"Oh, yeah," I said. "Those are great old songs."

But I decided to give her a lesson in really great old favorites the first chance I got. So one day when we were at home alone I got out my Ray Coniff album and turned it up to loud, the way she likes her music. He'd worked his way through "Someone to Watch Over Me" and was in the middle of "True Love" when she came out of her room groaning.

"Turn that off!" she pleaded, and the kid was in genuine pain.

"What's the matter?" I asked.

"That song–it reminds me of the dentist. That's the kind of stuff they play in the waiting room. It also reminds me of the time I had to go to the market for you–that last one was very big in the produce department."

I hadn't meant to conjure up such painful memories for her.

We have wrought–with our piped-in music in public places–a whole generation of kids who associate sentimental tunes with elevators, car washes and barber shops. Guilt, the middle-class parental hat, sits heavy on my head.

I'm sorry, kid, I really am, that when you and the man you finally choose sit down to your silver anniversary dinner by candlelight, you will have to reach over and cover his hand with yours when the band strikes up "Mack the Knife."

Forgive me for letting "YoYo" remind you of the best years of your life. When I should have been in your room smashing records, I was at the supermarket reliving my youth, dancing among the vegetables and corn flakes to "Sentimental Journey."

The gap may never close between our musical tastes, but do me a favor, will you? Keep that drummer you march to very distant.

The Illusion of Seclusion

When urban life becomes too much, when freeways, like huge strips of adhesive, fail to hold body and soul together, fear not.

Fear not, for there is always the mountain cabin. Or so I have been led to believe.

I read the ads. They promised me seclusion, nature, and silence broken only by the clear sweet song of the lark. I proceeded cautiously because I am not only cynical but thrifty.

I found the perfect spot. A truly lovely wooded lot at well below the market price. I haven't seen so many squirrels since my last family reunion.

But as my husband and I paced off the lot, I became increasingly nervous. I imagined every passing car was slowing down and memorizing the location preparatory to making a fatter offer than ours.

"Give the man our deposit," I urged my husband, "before it's too late."

And, good guy that he is, he wrote out a check. Aided and abetted by my hysterical attitude, he rushed about notching trees so we could find our way back to our property line. Soon, after a little pen pal interlude with the bank, we took possession.

And then the mail started coming in. "Hi, there!" said the first postcard. "Hear you're gonna be a mountaineer. Drop in and see us next time you're up." It was from an old friend of my husband's he hasn't seen in years who, it turned out, has retired just around the bend in our road.

Three acquaintances who have friends working in the escrow department of the bank wrote to say they had just broken ground a mile from us.

It turned into a postal cocktail party. "Listen," I said to my husband, "we had better build a big family room in our place. We won't have any family left by the time we build it, but think of all the friends who will be dropping by every 15 minutes. And where can we get glasses wholesale?"

He paled a little, put his arm around me and said, "Up

there, baby, it's just gonna be you and me." I'll admit I was relieved. If anybody knocks at our door, I'm not going to answer it–unless it's a squirrel.

Haven't I Seen You Somewhere Before? 🦋 I've always envied

people who can remember names but not faces–or faces but not names. At least they're half-safe; I forget everything.

Do you know what it's like to have a seemingly perfect stranger rush toward you at the supermarket and exclaim, "Hi, there!" Usually I'm so busy trying to pick out the best potatoes that I don't even notice until she grabs me by both shoulders and smiles into my dumbfounded face. Then I drop the potato and say something neutral, such as "Well, well."

And thereafter follows an excruciating little period during which my old pal asks me how all the members of my family are, calling them by name and remembering details about them even their doctor doesn't know.

It is very difficult for me to answer these questions with any show of alertness, as I am reaching into my memory bag trying to pull out an identity. Could it be my boy's teacher? Maybe. Could it be somebody I met at the party last week–in whom I confided more than I remember? Maybe.

Is it the mother of my daughter's girl friend with a new hairdo? Maybe.

Is it a crazy woman with ESP? I decide that it is and back away from her into the artichoke display. She follows, with alarming friendliness and concludes her reunion speech with a half question that screams for an answer: "You know how my husband is?" That's a pretty

wild question any way you look at it, so I do what Emily
Post would advise: confess all.

Extracting myself from the artichokes, I say with no
small amount of courage, "No, I don't. Give me a hint. Is
he a living American male? Is he fat? Is he bald? What
does he do for a living?" It is not the sort of response to
win friends and influence strangers. But it is honest.

Confronted with it, my friend is silent. And then she
rallies with, "Little League picnic. This spring. My son
pitches."

"Of course!" I scream, remembering how steady her
attendance was at every game and how much I admired
that. "What a kid! That Fred can really lay them in there!"
I exclaim.

She smiles patiently and reminds me, "His name is
Bobby." I am now clutching three artichokes for support
and trail off with. . . "How stupid of me . . ." But she is
the sort of woman who remembers her manners as well
as names and faces. "It happens to all of us," she says,
smiling.

I have a feeling it doesn't happen to her very often. But
I'll remember her the next time, I can tell you that—unless
she isn't wearing her red coat.

Hide and Seek at
Christmas 🐛 Christmas is for showing love and

hiding presents. For mothers, the hiding of presents can
be quite a challenge. Some mothers know how to keep a
kid guessing right up to the last minute. Will he get the
bike? The puppy? Will she get the admired doll?

Suspense in the heart of a ten-year-old can be exquisite
agony. Some mothers hide things so well that kids can
look with all their might, like terriers after truffles, and

find nothing but dust under the bed. Then the doubt sets in, and finally, on Christmas morning, the wished-for gifts appear from nowhere. With a flood of relief, shouts of "Merry Christmas!" escape from tiny throats that might otherwise have been permanently cramped with disappointment.

I loved that sort of suspense as a child, but unfortunately my mother hid things so poorly that it became my job to fake it after the first day of the hunt. Sometimes I didn't even have to hunt. My mother was fond of hiding presents in such places as the middle of the dining room table.

"Don't go into the dining room or you'll ruin your Christmas," she would say, and I would stand it as long as I could and then creep carefully in to find a big dollhouse. Then for two weeks I'd have to act excited and say things like, "Am I going to get my dollhouse, really and truly?"

Mother's reply was the same every year: "We'll see—if you behave yourself."

I wouldn't have denied her my mock anxiety and worried brow—it was part of her Christmas.

And when she delivered me from my supposed misery on Christmas morning, part of my fun was seeing her delight in thinking she had kept her secret.

So, mothers, hide those presents as best you can, but don't worry if somebody peeks. That's part of the fun.

Man and Supermarket 🐛 Food dollars

are buying less and less; I won't argue with the survey takers. Economists have ways of figuring things out, and I doff my hat to the mental giants who inform me that it will cost one-half of one percent more to fill the cornflake bowl from now on.

I just have a suggestion, that's all: keep husbands out of supermarkets.

It's not that our dollars are buying less; they're just buying the wrong things.

Only yesterday I saw a man behind a shopping cart with that married look. Pushing a toddler in a soggy diaper, he had a long shopping list in one hand and a worried look on his face.

"Can you tell me where I'll find the strained peaches?" he asked, as our shopping carts locked front wheels.

"Yes," I said. "Over there, down aisle A5–next to the imported foods."

Right away I knew I should never have told him. We were in paper goods at the time, and better he should wander in towels and tissues endlessly than go anywhere near that imported food section, because I'm willing to bet all my trading stamps that his poor toddler never sank its gums into any strained peaches once big daddy got a load of all those smoked oysters and roasted pumpkinseeds.

The last time I sent my husband to the market for a can of kidney beans, he came home with $15 worth of cheese and English crackers. That was twelve years ago, and he never has remembered the beans.

It is my guess that there was a lot more strained around that toddler's house than just peaches when mommy unpacked what her husband had brought home.

I can hear her now: "Danish herring? Frozen king crab? Chocolate-covered macadamia nuts? Where's my cooking oil, the peanut butter and the Tidy-bowl?" And back she went to the market.

Sending a husband may seem like a good idea at first, but it does cause the cost of living to rise.

If You Haven't Read It, Don't Wrap It

Books make wonderful gifts, but if you like to read, getting them wrapped may prove difficult. I recently bought for a friend's birthday a book I'd been wanting myself.

I tried to wrap it, I really did, but I made the mistake of reading the flyleaf. It was easy to go on to the introduction, and after that, of course, I was lost. I read chapter one wearing white gloves and turned the pages with a pair of tweezers. Heaven forbid that my friend should ever guess I had read the book first–robbing the pages of their virginity and rendering her gift used.

I finally gave it to her in pristine condition, but it wasn't easy. Chapter two was harder than chapter one, because I was tired of standing up. I had to be constantly on guard against curling up with it as it certainly was a good book. Snuggling makes the cover look tired.

Chapter three was a little easier because I discovered I could put down the tweezers and blow on the pages to turn them. But be careful about doing this while drinking coffee. Eating or drinking while sneak-reading is really out of the question, because it is disheartening to get as far as chapter twenty-seven, only to fleck melted chocolate on page 487. Or, worse yet, to drop graham cracker crumbs that will tumble out later to tell your friend what she might never have otherwise guessed.

And don't think you can let your guard down once she has received the book in perfect condition. After she reads it, your friend will be dying to tell you about it. You must feign surprise, interest and involvement as she unwinds the plot for you. Be careful about relaxing and saying, "I loved that part too."

Just keep nodding and saying things like, "Sounds as if you really enjoyed it." But don't tell her you'd like to read it or she'll offer to lend it to you.

Then you will have to sit down and read it over again—or at least try to make it look as if you did.

Knee-High to a Theater Ticket

🐝 Theater tickets, like trousers, should be sold by body measurements. Tall men and large women should sit in the last rows, unless they have bad eyes and can't afford glasses. In which case their closer tickets should be clearly marked "Slump Section," and if they sat upright during a performance, the usher could ask them to leave.

I think it's a sound idea, as any 5-foot-2 woman who has ever watched a stage from behind the neck of the big man in front of her would readily agree.

And don't tell me to lean to one side. I tried that and the lady next to me moved her purse to the other side. I leaned in the other direction and the man next to me leaned back.

There was a brief moment during the second act when the man in front of me bent forward to pick up his fallen program, and from what I saw then I think I liked the play.

I mean, I don't want to make snap judgments or anything, but it looked as though the stage crew had gone to a lot of trouble. You have to give credit where credit is due.

I liked the voices, too. Great lines, even if I wasn't sure who said them. During intermission I read the program in the lobby, and that helped.

And when I went back to my seat I cheated a little and sat on my purse. That's rough on your credit cards, but it sure gives you a nice clear view of the scrollwork above the stage. A reclining angel playing a trumpet, I think it was.

At any rate, the audience gave the play a standing ovation, and so did I. After all, I'd bought a ticket like everybody else, even though I wasn't properly measured for it.

But if anybody asks me if I saw that play, I'm not going to lie. "No," I'll say, "but I read the program."

Cleats and Cleavage 🐝 There's a new,

all-woman football team in New York called the Fillies and one of their players, a shapely blonde by the name of Gail Dearie, was recently referred to by a sportswriter as an "offensive end."

Is that any way to talk? Poor Gail, she probably does her best, but it's hard not to be offensive–especially to a man–when you're walking around in cleats and padded pants.

I can remember from my own days on the baseball diamond during high school that it is very easy to be offensive, even to one's own team. That's why they put me in the outfield: I was so offensive in the infield.

But the New York Fillies deserve all the reverence reserved for the Joe Namaths and the Jim Plunketts because these women are serious about football. Why should chauvinistic sportswriters give them labels like "offensive" and "defensive"?

You'd be defensive too, guys, if your shoulder pads were making sore spots on your collarbone that would show like anything when you wore your new off-the-shoulder formal. It's enough to make a woman edgy. Frankly, if the sportswriters and gagsters will lay off the Fillies, I think they have a darn good chance of winning the pennant. They may have to stop talking in the

huddles and become a little more forward with their
passes, but I think they can do it. Because women have
that tenacity, that sticking power that will put a team on
top every time.

I know that's how it was with me in the final game of
my high school championship baseball game. It was a
high pop fly, right out over my section of outfield. I ran
up on it, held my glove over my head and shut my eyes.
Neat as anything, the ball dropped right in, ending the
game in our favor.

Like the coach said, "It could only happen to a
woman." So, good luck, New York Fillies. Hang in there,
and don't worry about your sore collarbones—in a pinch
you could always wear your jersey to the party. Without
the shoulder pads, a jersey can be devastating on the
right quarterback.

The High Cost of
Not Going to Camp ❦ I don't know what
it's costing you to keep your child in camp, but whatever
it is, don't let him come home.

It will break you.

At first we thought we could only afford for our boy to
spend a week at the old "Lazy J," where, according to the
brochure, "boys and girls share the enriching experience
of a working ranch." But he was so enthusiastic, we
decided to extend ourselves and walk that narrow preci-
pice overhanging the depths of financial ruin. We made it.
And he made it.

He came home tanned and swaggering with a western
gait. He had also added two more four-letter words to his
vocabulary. But his fourteen-day experience with the great
outdoors didn't end when we unloaded his duffel bag of

dirty laundry from the back of the car. He went directly to his room, and I could tell by the look in his eyes that his soul was still hovering over the old "Lazy J."

"I want to have my guitar restrung," he said dreamily as he fingered the stringless instrument. "My counselor played a great guitar."

Feeling like one of Philip Wylie's moms, I turned to my husband and said, "My son is gone for two weeks, comes home, and instead of writing a sonnet to me and my cooking, he is camp-sick! 'How sharper than a serpent's tooth . . .' "

Fortunately for the boy's sake, my husband stopped me and gave the kid $4 to get his guitar restrung.

That was 10:30 in the morning. By noon all his friends had called, and three of them had invited him to their birthday parties. But the trouble is, when a friend hits eleven, he has everything in the toy store under $3, so it costs us another $12 to attend to his social life.

Then there was the two-week back allowance he figured we owed him. And the little debt he had to settle with the kid on the corner who had sold him a pair of real police handcuffs before he left for camp. But the event that really straightened him out and got him back in the swing of suburban living was the arrival of a community carnival.

There, amid the Ferris wheels, tilt-a-whirls and dime-throws, he managed to forget the joys of camp. And for only $37.23.

But I do have a black ceramic panther to show for it, and he gave his sister the stuffed snake he won. He could have stayed at the old "Lazy J" another week and we would have been $3 ahead.

Stuff That
Thanksgiving Turkey 🦃 Getting the family together for Thanksgiving is apt to be a thankless job. When the old familiar date rolls around, my family falls into two camps–both of which are pretty camp.

My Great-Aunt Minerva has been having Thanksgiving at her house for the last fifteen years, and any attempt on my part to change the tradition is enough to make her flip her pie tin. It will do me no good to tell her she is getting on and might enjoy being served for a change. She will only ask if it is because the potatoes were cold last year. She will say her house is bigger, her experience is greater, and nobody can do a turkey like she can.

She is right, of course, but what am I going to tell Grandma Harris, who for the last fifteen years has been trying to jockey Aunt Minerva off the turkey platter. Granny Harris is a good cook too. She has redecorated her living room in autumn tones and told the kids there will be a big surprise for them if grandma cooks the dinner on Thanksgiving.

Try to settle a contest like this.

Then there is the other reaction. The rest of my relatives think of reasons why they can't have Thanksgiving at their house. Cousin Debbie wishes she could, but she has only been married a year and her silver service consists of three forks and a sugar shell. Elwood and Ruth would, but they are in the middle of painting their kitchen (an event they planned to coincide with the cooking season).

The Murdocks had really planned on it, but little Freddie is due to come down with the measles that week. That leaves Uncle Harry, who is a bachelor, and me. Heaven knows, my intentions are the best, but with my tennis elbow how could I possibly lift a turkey into the oven? It's all I can do to lift the phone book and flip the yellow pages to "R" for restaurants. Or maybe I should try "M" for Minerva.

Taking Good Pictures Is No Snap 🐛 There is a TV commercial that worries

me every time I see it.

It's the one with the ethereal background music and the mother and dad taking pictures of a boy and girl as they grow up.

Suddenly the little girl is a young woman, the boy a man. But are mom and dad bereft? Not on your tintype.

They have a stack of snapshots showing each important moment in their children's lives, and all they have to do when they feel lonely is go to their files and look under "K" for kids.

The thing that worries me is, I'm no Richard Avedon. The pictures I take—when I take them—are apt to be overexposed or poorly balanced.

If I take a group of children, my kids are the ones on the end who get cut off. I'm either so far away that you can't tell who the kids are, or I'm so close I delete the tops of their heads. And I'm never there with the camera when I should be.

I got an impatient smile in front of my daughter's first bike, but I missed the look of joy when she pedaled off, hair flying, down the hill.

I arranged brother and sister side by side for a first-day-of-school picture, and it came out like a couple of hostages about to be shot. But I missed the way she took his hand at the corner to see that he got across the street safely.

At Christmas I take pictures of kids holding up merchandise, but I've never been able to get the look in their eyes as they sit around the fire on Christmas night.

I don't think changing cameras would help, but that commercial still worries me.

I'm afraid it may really be possible to catch the split-second image of childhood and I'm not doing it.

All I'm doing is seeing it, now and then, and trying not to forget.

So don't get in the way while I'm focusing on the way the sun hits that cowlick on the back of my boy's head. I'm taking a mind picture for future reference.

Throwing the Book at Overdue Offenders 🦋

Newspapers recently carried the story of a handful of very surprised people who had warrants issued for their arrests.

They were to be hauled into court for the heinous crime of keeping library books out too long.

Two of the eight people left town, probably leaving the books with a fence, and the rest of the group decided to face the music.

The last time I was in the library everybody looked innocent enough, but that only goes to prove you can't judge a book by its cover. Now that I think of it, there was an old man sitting in the corner reading a newspaper who looked as if he might be up to something. He kept looking over the top of the paper and rolling his eyes. At the time, I thought it was because my four-year-old was going through the card file, but now I'm not so sure.

And there was a very nervous woman sitting at a table reading. Every time my little boy shot off his gun, she jumped a foot. Would an innocent woman be so on edge? I think not. She probably had a record as long as your arm: three overdues, two counts of dog-earing, and checking out books with an expired card.

About the worst thing you could do in a library a few years ago was talk, but now if you have information about overdue books, the librarians encourage you to spill all. In fact, I understand the county will go easy on you for an overdue book if you welsh on three friends.

I never knew reading *Walden* could become so sordid, but then these are complex times we live in.

One aspect of the overdue scandal continues to bother me. What is to become of our young people if we allow them to hang out at the library? Pretty soon parents will narrow their eyes at their children when they come home an hour late from school and demand, "You haven't been to the library, have you?"

"No, pa, no," the teen-age boy will answer. "I've only been hanging around on street corners."

"Thank goodness," dad will sigh.

As well he might. No telling what may happen to the boy should he decide to check out a book.

Alarms To Ring Your Bell 🌰 Telephones have become electronic wonders, with direct distance dialing and built-in night lights, but why hasn't someone done something about the lowly alarm clock?

It still wakes people up with a sound that can only be compared to a bronx cheer. It's rude the way mine goes off. No preamble, no warning, just–POW!

Don't tell me about radio-alarms, because I don't think it's much better to wake up to a commercial. What I'd like to see is some scientist given a grant to develop an alarm clock that would wake people up personally–with feeling.

Instead of ringing, it could talk to the sleeper so he would really want to get up. Clocks could come with three different built-in talks; depending on the sleeper's hangup, he would select the one most likely to get a rise out of him.

Model A–the guilt alarm–would say, "Okay, buddy, you've slept seven hours, and what have you got to show for it? You could have been washing your car or waxing the floor for your wife. If you get up right now, you'll have time to make it up by skipping breakfast and mowing the lawn." Guaranteed to get the guilty up.

Model B would be the regression alarm. It would say, in a motherly voice, "Time to get up, precious. If you don't want to you don't have to, but there's something nice waiting for you in the bottom of your cereal bowl. A picture of Jane Fonda." Maybe the scientist could work out a bottle of warm milk with this one.

The model C alarm is the one I'd need: the anxiety model. "Do you realize what time it is?" it would say. "You have only eight hours today to do 254 things. Get up right away or you will have to drive the kids to school in your underwear again. Hurry! Hurry!"

It's not that I don't want to get up; it's just that I need convincing. And a raucous ring is no way to do it. Ordinary clocks are alarming.

Follow the Bouncing Baby Boy 🐝 I baby-sat an

eighteen-month-old boy for a friend of mine last week, and I fail to see why it's called baby-sitting. I didn't sit down once.

Little Eddie reminded me what it is like to tangle with a toddler. I thought I had problems trying to keep my older kids out of adult movies, but Eddie had to be kept out of everything.

I spent the afternoon staying between him and everything within reach. He loves ashtrays (especially full ones), decanters, vases, potted plants and lamps. If he couldn't reach it, he went after it with all the dexterity of King Kong up the Empire State.

Eddie found cupboards I didn't know I had.

All it takes to keep up with a kid like this is a reach like Too Tall Jones, legs like Dave Waddle, and the eye of a white hunter. The only time he sat down was when I gave him my wedding pictures. "See the bride!" I said enthusiastically. He sat right down–and tore them up.

But it took him seven minutes, and that was long enough for me to lie down on my slant board and think things out. It was then I remembered naps. Toddlers take naps. But Eddie didn't want to sleep in unfamiliar surroundings–not unless he could snuggle up on my white taffeta bedspread with a bottle of orange juice and a chocolate cookie.

That left the bunk bed for me, but I couldn't have cared less. I was asleep in 18 seconds. It took Eddie 22 seconds to finish his bottle, his cookie and my bedspread. He got right down off the bed, found me in the other room, and surveyed me critically.

Was I asleep, or wasn't I?

To make sure, he lifted my eyelid. Sure enough, I wasn't.

When his mother came for him, she said she hoped he hadn't been any trouble.

"He was an angel," I said. But then, so was Beelzebub–once.

The Million-Dollar Want Ad 🐛 If Liz

Taylor beat you to the Krupp diamond and you've lost all hope for the Hope, don't give up entirely.

The Idol's Eye, a 70-karat blue-white diamond, has just been put on the market by its owner, Chicago jeweler Harry Levinson. And it's "on sale." No fooling.

Levinson decided that at seventy-one he is, as he put it, "at an age where I might want to retire pretty soon."

Harry's in a hurry, and we all stand to benefit, because he can't afford to waste time waiting for the right people to make an offer on the Idol's Eye. He wants action and he wants it now, so Harry put an ad in a Chicago newspaper announcing that he is going to let the huge diamond go for only $1 million.

Levinson says he doesn't see anything unconventional about selling the diamond necklace through a classified ad. "Why, I sell things that way all the time," he said.

I believe you, Harry. I sold a chest of drawers and my husband's golf clubs that way, and not only did I get my price, but my phone never stopped ringing, and I really felt popular.

You're going to feel that way too, Harry, because I for one am going to call you for further details. I mean, if my husband says I can come over and try it on, I'll be there.

I don't know what wearing a diamond of that weight would do to my posture.

I won't mislead you: if it makes me round-shouldered, I'll have to pass it up. Nothing's a bargain if it isn't becoming. But I could always carry it in my purse, or use it as a paperweight.

My Son the What-Mom 🐛 I'm not

much of a bird watcher, but we have, nesting at our house, a species the Audubon Society would undoubtedly classify as a bird of prey.

He is the North American what-mom, and he is making mincemeat of my nervous system. The what-mom is characterized by his blatant call, from which he gets his name–"What-mom? What-mom?"

If you are trying to coax a what-mom into your house, or from one room to another, just get on the phone and say, "Really? Isn't that interesting." The what-mom will fly right in, jiggle your arm and say, "What-mom? What-mom?"

Or you might try sitting down with your husband when he comes home after a brisk swim in the car pool and try to have a 15-minute cocktail hour.

After the first three sips, when you think your husband is ready for it, you can summon the what-mom by saying, "I don't want the kids to know this, but . . ." And there he will be, in the brilliant plumage of his baseball shirt, with that familiar call: "What-mom? What-mom?"

And this bird is always on hand when you are trying to decide whether to take the kids out to dinner with you or to go alone for the full treatment. He will pop out of the bush the minute he hears the word hamburger–which brings me around to the what-moms' eating habits.

For their size, they put away quite a bit: I'd say about two-thirds of your week's grocery allowance. What-moms are big on peanut butter, filled cookies, grape soda and beef jerky. Don't try to get a what-mom to eat anything that might be good for you or me, because he prefers high-calorie, low-food-value foods.

And the really sickening thing about what-moms is that they are skinny even though they eat twelve meals a day. What-moms are very active and are apt to play outside until dark unless you remember to call them in. They have poor hearing, however, and once they are involved in doing something they enjoy, you can stand on your front porch and holler a what-mom's name for as long as your strength lasts.

He won't come home. But he might answer you–from forty blocks away–"What-mom? What-mom?"

It's No Picnic on the Freeway

🐞 One of the things I have against freeways is that there's no place to pull over for a picnic. The closest thing I've seen to a shady spot is the shadow cast by the emergency phone.

Part of the fun of going on a picnic when I was a kid was not knowing where we were going to stop–looking for a "good spot" on a meandering road.

But with hardly any meandering roads left, a family goes on a picnic today something like this: the kids make out a shopping list for mom with all the things they've seen on TV that are bad for their teeth. While she is at the store stocking up, dad drives over to the take-out chicken restaurant and buys a bucket full of mostly wings.

Then they all pile into the car and argue about which freeway to take. Mother wants the San Diego South because she hopes the brakes will go out and they will all end up in Mexico. Dad wants the Airport Norwalk Freeway because it hasn't been built yet and he can say he can't find it and go home and eat the chicken on his patio.

The kids want the Harbor Freeway because it passes a drive-in theater and they hope they'll come home late enough to catch a glimpse of *Apocalypse Now.*

They compromise and take the Santa Monica East; and while dad looks out for merging traffic, mom and the kids look out for a patch of green or a tree.

"Hey, look!" says the youngest. "There's a good place."

It is a miniature golf course.

"There's a nice spot," says mom, who is getting sick of holding the Twinkies.

"Where?" asks dad, and mom answers, "Now you've missed the turn-off! If you'd been alert we could have picnicked beside the bill-board down there with the picture of a lovely lake on it."

But things have a way of working out if you just give them time. The left rear tire blows out and they pull over to fix it.

There, by the edge of the freeway, they eat the picnic, while car after car whizzes by—oblivious to them.

One thing you have to say for people in the big city: they will not disturb a family picnic. That would be an invasion of privacy.

It Isn't a Bargain
If You Need It ✌ Men may wait for open

season on pheasant or deer, but for women, the first "clearance" sign is the equivalent of the hunter's horn.

During all those dreary weeks before spring, we ladies can occupy ourselves with the exciting pursuit of something for less. Is there anything more attractive than a shopworn irregular sweater the wrong size in a color you never wear?

If you can't use it, buy it for your neighbor who is a shut-in. She, poor thing, cannot get out to join in the togetherness of traffic jams and the intimacy of breath-filled elevators.

The sweater will take her mind off the cruel fact that she was felled in her prime last year by a body blow in ladies' ready-to-wear while fighting for a pair of damaged dungarees.

But philanthropy is only one excuse for hitting the sale circuit. Don't forget the good, sound sense of business most women have.

I am particularly talented at ferreting out financial opportunities in the morning paper. Like that tiny six-column ad I saw the other day offering me a chance to buy a $3,900 horizontal mink coat for a mere $2,500. I can't think of a better way to render my husband horizontal than to take advantage of such an ad.

So I have to be careful to buy big bargains on a small scale—like that case of hominy at two cents off a can.

I saved enough on that deal to take us all out to dinner for a week so we wouldn't have to eat it.

That's thinking, and it proves that sales do make sense. They're good for the country's economy, and they keep women moving so they won't get obese. Or at least if they do, they can buy something to wear in a bigger size so no one will notice.

Staying Ready for Christmas 🐛

"Christmas is coming . . ." the ad warned, but I didn't fall for it. Because, starting the day after Christmas, when isn't it coming?

I used to think the man next door was lazy when he left his outdoor Christmas lights strung to his roof until after Easter; now I know he was only previous. He knew what it was all about and should not have listened to the urgings of his neighbors who told him to take down those ridiculous lights.

A lot they knew. They are the very ones who spend the last free weekend before Christmas climbing around their eaves hanging lights in the rain.

And people who send me cards on December 26—it's not because I mailed them one on December 23. No, sir. These people are on their toes. By sending out cards the day after Christmas, nobody knows if they are late or early, and they kill two years with one card. Clever, that's what it is.

Same thing with post-holiday sales. Why slacken your pace and stop shopping just because Christmas was yesterday? You're in shape now for the rest of the year—alert and ready. You know how to give a rabbit punch to anybody who might try to edge in front of you at the gift box counter, and you can remember quite clearly what everybody you're shopping for gave you just yesterday.

Simply hop into your car twelve hours after your Christmas dinner has digested and head for the nearest shopping center. All it takes is a little planning and you too can get ahead of Christmas.

But if you want to celebrate it, you have to go back. Back about 2,000 years to a manger where there were no Christmas lights–only one guiding star above. And there was no price tag on love.

Groceries Groceries Everywhere, and Not a Bite To Eat 🍎 Progressive

Grocer, a trade magazine, reports that the average American family buys 6,700 pounds of groceries a year.

They are all carried home by housewives in 36 billion brown paper bags. I believe the bag part, because in my kitchen cupboard I have 200 bags from last week alone.

But I find that 6,700 pounds of groceries a little hard to swallow. I think it is just one more unfair blow to the American housewife's image. Insurance companies have been harping for years about the few extra pounds of weight the average woman carries, and now along come the grocers to say, "No wonder. She totes home 6,700 pounds of food a year."

Sure, I'll admit to the 272 million trips to the check-out stands they accuse me of, but don't try to tell me it's food I'm buying.

Ask my kids. "Gee, mom," they say every day after school, "how come you never have anything good in the house?"

I can stagger through the back door under three bags of groceries and still not have anything for dinner. I unload such delectables as ammonia, detergent, paper towels and matches.

But the way those grocers talk, you'd think I was a compulsive eater. Just check my bag, fellas; it's full of window cleaner, dog food and presto-logs. I swear it. I haven't had a square meal since the PTA potluck.

I don't care if grocers have kept track of my cash register tape–1,003,600 miles of it, they say; it's all spray starch and foaming cleanser. If I've been a glutton, it's been for aluminum foil and waxed paper.

Say I've gone overboard for patio candles and paper cups, or accuse me of overbuying disposable dust-cloths, but please, Mr. Grocer, when it comes to 6,700 pounds of food, don't leave me holding the bag.

From Little Girl to New Woman 🐝 Our little girl has disappeared

and I'm thinking of turning in a missing persons report.

I'm only thinking about it, because the young lady we have in her place is really quite charming–at times. At thirteen she doesn't have the wispy ponytails she used to have on either side of her head, and she is definitely too big to hold on my lap, but she's a lot more fun to talk to.

At three she could say, "Give me the red crayon." At thirteen, she can say, "Art is what you believe it is."

And she is certainly a lot more fun to watch. At three I took her to dancing school. At thirteen she takes me–she knows all the latest dances. My attempts to learn them have kept my sense of humor–and my spine–limber. And she can empty a dishwasher, make her own bed, and return overdue library books for me.

But, that three-year-old never used my perfume, wore my shoes or said, "Oh, mother!" the way she does.

The little girl had a plastic phone she liked just fine. The thirteen-year-old has a hot line to six girl friends. The pre-schooler was always ready to help in the kitchen–spilling flour, dropping eggs, and sprinkling sugar on the floor. But the thirteen-year-old has better things to do. There is her hair to put up and the first tentative strokes of lipstick to apply and judo class.

Sometimes, when the big girl is asleep, I can see the little girl–in the soft curve of her cheek; or perhaps she lurks among the dolls and stuffed toys that still adorn her bed.

And I whisper good-bye to the little girl that was. But hello too. Hello and welcome to a girl as new as tomorrow.

Movement Very Slow
South of the Border 🦋 Down in Rio de

Janeiro, the women's movement has suffered a serious setback after an apparently giant step forward.

It seems that Claudiote Vasconcelos, the only woman to be elected to the Chamber of Aldermen in Rio Largo, is having a little trouble getting the guys to open up and let her in.

The men have locked her out of the chamber, and it's no wonder. They are the same fellows responsible for Rio Largo's famous saying, "A woman may open her mouth in her husband's presence for only three reasons–to scold the children, to call the chickens, and to cry for help if her husband is trying to kill her."

Claudiote, dear, I don't know what to suggest, unless you want to resort to devious methods. I mean, you could always stand outside the chamber door and call a few chickens, and when the boys opened up to see what the racket was about, you could slip right by them and into the room before any of them could slam the door.

But I don't know. Once you gained entry using that method, it would be pretty awkward for you to contribute much unless your husband was an alderman too and he tried to strangle you.

Then, of course, your problems would be solved. You could open your mouth all you wanted and nobody could stop you without looking like a male chauvinist pig.

Or it may be that your only hope is the scolding-the-children clause. Get yourself down to that chamber before any of the men arrive and be dressed like everybody's mother figure.

You know the bit, Claudiote. No tweeds, no tailored jackets—just pure mom all the way down the line. A voile housedress, cardigan sweater around your shoulders, and a basket of homemade cookies over your arm.

By the time any of them recognize you, you'll be inside the chamber and scolding. And when those aldermen go home at night, frustrated, tired, and all on edge from listening to you, a lot of them will try to kill their wives.

Just think, Claudiote, those women will have you to thank for giving them a chance to speak up. You've come a long way, baby.

Mechanics of Equality 🦋 One of the benefits of the women's movement is that now a woman can do things for herself that she formerly had to depend on a man for.

Take car maintenance. It used to be that I'd ask my husband, "Do I need oil?" and he'd say, "How should I know? Ask the guy at the garage."

Then I'd drive my car to the corner gas station and ask a big hulk of a fellow the same question.

He never really gave me a direct answer—he would raise my car hood, take a deep bow into the engine, and then approach my open car window with a long metal wand and show me the end of it which he had cradled on a dirty rag.

I'd look at it dumbly and say, "Well?" and he'd control himself with effort and say between clenched teeth, "Lady, yer down two quarts. Ya want 30 weight?"

I always sensed, and rightly so, I feel, that if I asked him what did he mean by weight, he might do me harm—or at the very least snap the metal wand in two.

Now all that has changed. If I wanted to, I could go to night school and learn auto mechanics. And my corner gas station now takes a few cents off the price if a driver pumps his or even her own. And though I haven't taken the night school mechanics, just knowing I could has given me the confidence I need to drive in and belly up to the gas pumps.

As I was filling my own tank recently, I looked over at the guy filling his own on the next gas island and said, "Who do you favor in the fight tonight? I like Indian Red Lopez for a TKO in the fifth."

I haven't felt so equal since I flattened Johnnie Doolittle with my lunch bucket in the third grade after he blew chalk dust in my face.

Of course, I'm still not sure if I need oil or not, but I'm working on it.

If I'd Known You Were Coming, I'd Have Locked the Door 🐝 We all

know her: she's the housewife whose cupboards are

organized, whose copper cooking pots look as new as the day she bought them.

She is able, somehow, to keep her kids' tee shirts white-white, and there are no fingerprints on her polished coffee table. Not only that–she takes naps.

I long ago stopped trying to figure out her modus operandi, but I am ever on the alert for her visits. Her visits are what keep me from outdoing the FBI when it comes to fingerprints.

I say to myself, "Look at those peanut butter prints all over the kitchen wall! What if Elvira should drop in and see them?"

Just the thought of it sends me up the wall after those tiny finger tracks.

Once I get going, of course, Elvira stays with me. She isn't an easy woman to shake. She peeks over my shoulder approvingly when I occasionally scour my frying pan vigorously, and covers her face in despair when I sling it with abandon, smoky-black, into my chaotic cupboard with all my other less-than-perfect cooking gear.

Elvira is the woman who drops in on you unexpectedly the morning after a late dinner party when you have wall-to-wall glasses in the living room, full ashtrays and a sinkful of dirty dishes.

And when you try to clear a place for her to sit down, mumbling apologies, she is also the woman who says, "Don't be silly! You should see my place–it's an absolute mess!"

But she's taking it all in, and even though you swallow three cigarette butts and manage to throw five dirty glasses out the window when she isn't looking, you know damn well her place is as antiseptic as ever.

What she means by a "mess" is that two of her sofa pillows are pointing south instead of the customary north. Another friend of mine remarked with admiration last week that Elvira's kitchen floor is so clean you could eat off it.

Maybe that's her secret—they do eat off it. What a way to save dishwashing! And think how neat your cupboards would stay! That has to be it.

Crazy Like a Woman ❦ I've never been

quite able to articulate why I think a lot of learning is a dangerous thing for a woman—one of the penalties, no doubt, of not having a lot of learning.

But I have always felt, instinctively, that a woman is better off just this side of dimwitted.

For one thing, she can put a lot more creative energy into things like cleaning corners and scraping dried eggs off the stove if her mind isn't cluttered with thoughts of—well—thoughts, period.

Being a bit thick has many advantages, I've found. Like the night when my son was doing a ten-page report on the Middle East crisis. He was sitting at the kitchen table looking like Nasser in a Hang Ten shirt.

"Want a marshmallow?" I asked gaily, and he turned dark and brooding eyes upon me.

"How can you ask me that when Jordan is in the fix it's in?" he asked.

I popped the marshmallow into my mouth and dropped an arm around his shoulder. "I know how you feel," I said, chewing. "Want me to help you with your 3,000-word report?"

"You?" he asked incredulously, remembering, no doubt, what a whiz I am at dried eggs on stoves. "Ma, this has got to be a really good report!"

Well, of course that let me out right away.

A boy's mother may be able to get grass stains out of his pants, but that doesn't mean she knows how to get Israel out of Egypt.

I may not agree with my son on whether or not he

should tuck in his shirt, but I do concur wholeheartedly with him that homework is his bag and should not be rummaged in by me.

Darn it all, I'll just have to sit down somewhere, put my feet up, sip a little coffee and finish reading *The French Lieutenant's Woman*. That's what I get for being stupid.

The New Wave Motel 🍎 What's happened to motels has been so gradual it's hard to remember when they were called auto courts. But I do.

Auto courts were no great shakes, but then neither were cars in those days. Auto courts had linoleum floors, creaky bed springs, faded curtains, and towels you wouldn't want to use—let alone steal.

Now, of course, all that has changed. Motels are not just $1.50 places to sleep on your way somewhere; they are an experience.

Last week my husband and I were driving along trying to decide which motel to choose from a line of them that boggled the eye. They all had flashing marquees out front advertising the delights to be had inside.

Waterbeds, continental breakfasts and—no kidding—first-run movies in your room.

Unfortunately, we had our twelve-year-old along. Had we been alone, we would have been content with a standard room, with a standard bed at a standard price. But a twelve-year-old boy is straining at the bit to experience all. "Wow!" he yelled from the backseat. "Waterbeds! Movies!"

"Now look," I said, assuming my Scout leader expression, "we are stopping here for a good night's rest and no nonsense."

That sounded pretty dull, even to me, so I weakened. "OK, if the movie is nonviolent and sexless, we'll watch it–but from a real bed. No water. I didn't drive 200 miles to fight tidal waves all night."

Once we were inside the room, however, there were other diversions.

"Turn on the TV and give me a quarter so I can make the bed vibrate," said the twelve-year-old.

I dropped a quarter into a slot on the nightstand, and his bed began to hum and quiver. He was in ecstasy.

I sat down and contemplated the rest of the room while my husband struggled with the luggage. The beds were huge, the pictures were huge, the lamps were huge. And everything that could possibly be lifted by anybody ambulatory had been bolted down. It was a silent indictment of past visitors.

"Isn't this n-n-neat?" asked my vibrating son, and I said yes. No sense in spoiling his fun. It's not that I miss auto courts; it's just that there really is no place like home.

Why Do You Treat Me Like You Voodoo Do? 🦋 What is a mother-in-law? Besides being the mother of your husband, she is also a woman whose cooking, housekeeping and general habits are viewed, across the nostalgic years, by a son who is married to a real live girl.

And that's dynamite.

Ask any real live girl. A mother-in-law is somebody who tells you she is coming to visit on Tuesday and then pops in on Monday when you are getting ready for her by scrubbing the kitchen floor in your old college sweat shirt. She is somebody who sends you a size 14 when you wear a 10. "Honestly, dear, I described you to the salesgirl." She tells your husband you ought to have a full-time maid because you look tired. But she is all heart, and all you have to do is to get sick for her to prove it.

"When you get home from the hospital," your husband announces, "mom will be here." Talk about voodoo–you can hardly speak, and you haven't even had the operation yet.

Before you go to the hospital, you clean the house from top to bottom and throw out all the empty peroxide bottles. You're ready for her.

But during your five-day stay in the hospital, your husband and two kids have been fending for themselves. Your mother-in-law walks into a house with wall-to-wall dirty socks, a sink full of dishes and a son with three buttons missing.

Could any mother ask for more? It only takes her two days to get things back in shape. Two days and six high-calorie meals: "Eat it, dear, it will do you good."

By the time she leaves, you can wear that size 14 she bought for you. But your strength is returning, and you can manage–just barely–to prop yourself up on one elbow and inform your husband: "No wonder your mother's meals always melt in your mouth–she doesn't thaw those TV dinners."

To be honest, it is rather nasty of you. But never mind, you can buy her something nice for Christmas.

The Joy of
Christmas Loaning 🐝 If you think you
have problems deciding what to buy Great-Aunt Zelda, who has everything, just wait until your child decides he wants to buy Christmas presents for everybody with his very own money. He rushes into the kitchen one morning after your gifts have already been bought and wrapped and enclosure cards signed with his name on them.

"Mom!" he shouts. "I've got a great idea!"

"Yeah?" you answer warily. You remember the last time he had a great idea.

"I'm gonna buy all my own gifts this year!" he announces. Then he whips out a list he has compiled with thirty-six names on it. Wiping the fruitcake mix from your hands, you come on like Scrooge: "Wait just a minute, Diamond Jim. How much money have you got?"

He is still soaring on the spirit of Christmas go-for-broke when he answers, "Lots–$18.36, and I'm gonna spend it all." It is then that your heart softens (a lapse you will live to regret) and you say, "I think that is wonderful of you, Freddie." Nevertheless, you are mentally calculating that $18 into thirty-six people comes out only 50 cents apiece. But you leave your fruitcake preparations, bundle up and drive him down to the local five-and-ten. There, you turn him loose with instructions to watch his budget and meet you in an hour, after he has made his selections. You can't help but wonder how the kid is going to handle it. You spend the next hour loitering in the supermarket, then go back to pick him up. But he is emptyhanded.

"Where are all your presents?" you ask.

"I couldn't find anything," he answers. "For 50 cents the five-and-ten had nothing but thermos corks and bath salts that make you itch like anything. I need a two-year advance on my allowance. I'll pay ya back–I promise." His eyes are shining like two Christmas stars, and you realize there is nothing to say but yes. So you say it.

And on Christmas morning you're glad you did, for there's a light in Great-Aunt Zelda's eyes as she holds the $1.49 pot holder Freddie gave her. "You picked this out yourself, didn't you?" she asks.

"Yes," says Freddie proudly, and you know he has felt the joy of giving. Even if he does owe his soul to the company store.

Public Speaking, Private Fears 🦋 According to a recent survey,

Americans' No. 1 fear is public speaking. But like all
surveys, it gives figures but no solutions.

Having delivered my share of quivering speeches, I can
tell you the key to mike fright is not coping but prevention. The last time I stood before a suddenly quiet group
and looked down at my notes only to discover somebody
had rewritten them in Arabic, I made up my mind: never
again.

I don't even remember what I finally said; I only know I
did a lot of heavy breathing into the microphone between
sentences. When I finished, I lost my way back to my
seat, which was right behind me.

"Ha, ha," I said mirthlessly to anybody who would
listen. "There's my seat now."

But the next speaker was already holding forth, and she
was obviously one of those minority percentages who
aren't the least bit frightened of speaking before a group.

In fact, she was even able to let go of the dais and
gesture with one hand to emphasize a point.

I'm not sure, but I think she's the same kid, grown up,
who used to sit behind me in the sixth grade and had all
the answers to the oral arithmetic quizzes.

But, as I say, the solution to such public pain is
prevention. All the way home in the car, after I had given
my speech perfectly to myself and even let go of the
wheel to gesture with one hand, I thought of things to
say the next time somebody asks me to speak.

One of the quickest turn-offs is that you charge. Or you
might tell them your subject will be a complete history of
your tennis elbow and how you are feeling now.

You could tell them you'd love to speak, and not to pay
any attention to the rumors that your ex-husband is

looking to gun you down first chance he gets.

And if you're ever caught offguard and pressed into service for "a few words" after dinner, just stand up and tell them the truth: "I think I'm gonna be sick."

Floored by an Elevator 🍎 The self-service elevator has risen from a rickety budget-cutter found only in second-rate apartment houses to a perfectly acceptable way to shoot up fifty stories.

It's too late now to wish for the return of the kindly old elevator man–he with the friendly smile and solicitous inquiry into the state of your health. He was particularly comforting in the medical building elevators.

While riding up seven stories to your dental appointment, you could talk to him to ease your tension, and if the car was empty you might even point out the troublesome tooth.

Now you have to ride alone. As you slide silently up, keeping one ear cocked for the sound of snapping cables, your problem is greater than a throbbing bicuspid. You're really not too worried about its falling: there hasn't been a story in the newspapers for months about an elevator falling.

But they stall all the time. As for that red emergency button, how do you know it works? With the elevator out of order, it would be the same as dialing the operator to ask why your phone is dead.

If it does stall, you can keep calm for a time by going through your wallet. Get rid of those expired credit cards, grow nostalgic over that snapshot of you and Herbert when you were both thin. There's plenty of time to beat on the doors and scream when the building is ready to close and people are going home for the weekend.

The next best thing to a kindly elevator man is a fellow

passenger who looks as if he might be a brain surgeon, an astronaut, or someone equally qualified to keep calm under pressure. If you are good at snap judgments, look over the waiting passengers, get in with one who falls into the well-adjusted category, and let him push the buttons.

Never, if you can help it, get into a self-service elevator with women holding small dogs, teen-agers in groups of more than two, men in gray fedoras carrying violin cases, or pregnant women in their ninth month. You can if you want, of course; but without the kindly old elevator man to keep things under control, anything might happen before you reach your floor.

As for me, I'll take the stairs.

I'm Running, but Not Late 🐛

There's a man in Indiana whom I admire greatly. I don't know him but I've read about him. He returned a library book that was forty-five years overdue. There's a fellow who isn't uptight about schedules.

Would that I could hang so loose. But not me. If I have a doctor's appointment for 10 o'clock, I'm there fifteen minutes early.

And where is the doctor? Somewhere in his labyrinth of consulting rooms, under stress, I'm sure, but nevertheless an hour and a half behind schedule.

I'd hate to be bleeding to death out there in the waiting room with nothing for a tourniquet but the latest copy of the *National Geographic*.

It's the same thing with meetings. If the notice from school says be there at 3:30 because we are going to decide what to do about the sump in the middle of the school yard, I'm there. I'm there at 3:30 even though I have my dress on backwards and didn't have time to brush my teeth.

But where is everybody else? Did I read the notice wrong? No, it's the right day, but meetings are like cocktail parties–they really don't get going until they are almost over.

Then madam president will stand up and say, "Since we didn't have time to cover everything in today's meeting, we will meet again next week."

I've found it isn't essential to cover everything at a meeting–just my ears. Or else I'll hear what time I'm supposed to be there next week.

I really don't know how that man in Indiana with the overdue book managed to play it so cool. I'm afraid of librarians and always have been–I couldn't have held out for more than two weeks at the most.

But forty-five years! If I thought I could get away with that sort of thing gracefully, I'd check out *War and Peace* and finish it.

Apple Pie–Almost ❦ When my daughter

announced she had to do 20 hours of cooking at home as part of her high school homemaking assignment an involuntary sob of joy escaped me.

After years in the kitchen, I was to get a reprieve. However short, I was elated.

That was before I saw her in action. She sent me to the market with a list of things to buy which, I am sure, could have fed King Farouk for two years.

"How come you need all this stuff?" I asked. I didn't want to look a gift cook in the mouth, but twenty-seven apples for a pie did seem rather excessive.

"Mother," she said, helping me out of the kitchen by my elbow, "just let me handle the pie my own way."

"What else are we having for dinner?" I pressed; standing firm and refusing to be lowered onto the sofa. She had both hands on my shoulders now and was looking into my eyes like a kid about to rebel.

"It's going to be a surprise," she said firmly, and I knew she was in charge. That is to say, she was in charge of me.

As for dinner, the surprise was that she was going to cook that next week.

She was in the kitchen with those twenty-seven apples four hours and finally emerged carrying what I must admit was a handsome apple pie.

Behind her, the kitchen was a disaster area. There was flour everywhere—even at the end of her nose.

"It's a beautiful pie, dear," I said.

"Really?" she asked. "Do you think he will like it?"

"Daddy will love it," I assured her.

"Oh, it isn't for him," she answered nonchalantly. "It's for my boyfriend."

You could have knocked me over with a rolling pin. "What about us?" I whined.

"Oh, I'll make you some applesauce—I have a lot of apples left over," she said, as she tenderly wrapped the pie in waxed paper.

It was marvelous applesauce, because it took her three hours to make it. Let's see, four hours for the pie, three for the applesauce—only 13 more hours and I can have my kitchen back.

Santa, You Made the Tree Too Tall 🦋 We made a terrible mistake last

year. We took the kids with us when we picked out the Christmas tree.

If there is one thing kids do not understand about Christmas trees, it is that they are sold by the foot. Our son didn't care what the proportions were, as long as it hit the ceiling. Not our ceiling, the ceiling of La Scala Opera House.

We could always cut off the extra fifty feet—he just wanted the biggest tree on the lot. Our daughter was more aesthetic.

"Mom," she said, with great understanding, "I know size isn't the most important thing."

"Good girl!" I said.

She slipped her arm through mine in a gesture which I should have immediately recognized as compromising and led me toward a row of trees that had been sprayed, flecked, and otherwise defiled by commercial methods.

"These trees are much smaller—and I have always wanted a pink Christmas tree," she confided, squeezing my wrist.

If it had been $2, I would have bought a brown one.

"It is rather unusual," I said, and reached for the price tag. I won't tell you what they wanted, but very few people had a pink Christmas that year.

I squeezed her wrist back and said "That's more than I'm spending on your father." In the meantime, father was trying to talk our son out of a eucalyptus tree which just happened to be growing near the edge of the lot.

I caught my husband's eye the way I do when I want to leave a party early. Both of us gravitated toward the car with son and daughter in tow. Overhead, a loudspeaker blared, "Santa Claus Is Coming to Town."

I certainly hope he is, because I want to speak to him.

I'd Love To, But
My Hands Aren't Up to It 🦋 You've

seen it, I'm sure—the commercial showing a group of
teen-agers having fun, unaware that an imposter is in
their midst.

The imposter is a thirty-year-old woman who, because
she uses a certain hand lotion, has managed to pass for a
teen-ager.

I hate to disappoint the laity of Madison Avenue, but,
hand lotion or no hand lotion, most thirty-year-olds today
look good enough to pull off that sort of impersonation
very nicely. What I'm waiting for is a lotion that will
allow an over-forty to fit in with the kids. After all, we
are the ones who need to keep an eye on our children.

I can see it now: I hear that the kids are all going down
to the beach for a cookout. Quickly I slosh on a few drops
of hand lotion and jump into my jeans.

Immediately my daughter says, "Mom! I love your
hands. Come with us to the beach."

"Cool!" I reply, doing the skate down the hall, and she
takes me aside for a girl-to-girl talk.

"Look, mom," she says. "Lay off with the skate. It's
out. Do the disco or stand still."

Crestfallen but still game, I do the disco out to the
waiting car and jump into the backseat. It is not a rumble
seat, so I slide off into the gutter.

But kids today are very tolerant and broad-minded, so
they overlook it. Besides, they are crazy over my hands.

We get to the beach and I am alert for signs of
debauchery. But the boys run off to play football and the
girls gather in a close circle to discuss the merits of electric
hair rollers as opposed to curling irons.

I count the hot dogs and discover we are going to be
twelve short.

"Children," I begin, and amend it to, "Hey, you guys," but nobody pays any attention. The boys have come back and everybody starts singing around the fire.

I jump into the car and run to the market for two more packages of hot dogs. When I get back they all eye me carefully and say, "How come you're so efficient?"

For a minute I think the jig is up, but I break into a mad disco and all is saved.

The truth is, however, that as the evening wears on— and on—it would probably be harder and harder to keep up with my hands. The rest of me is exhausted, but my hands and those kids never seem to tire.

And, very frankly, even if there were a lotion that would allow me to fit in with the kids, I'd be better off pouring it down the sink.

I think I'll wait for one that will make my hands look older. It's respect and reverence I'm after.

There's No Excuse for a Plumber 🦋 We never call a plumber until whatever is wrong threatens to overflow into a public health problem.

And it certainly isn't my fault. The minute I saw signs of trouble I'd reach for the Yellow Pages, but I happen to be married to a man who is very handy around the house. With an excuse.

"Never mind about that little problem in the children's bathroom," he will say cheerfully over his morning eggs. "I'll fix it first chance I get."

Anybody who has ever had a little problem in the children's bathroom will understand my panic at contemplating any sort of delay.

"When?" I'll ask anxiously, leaning forward and grip-ping the table edge for support.

"Soon's I get a wrench," he will answer, smiling ami-ably.

It is possible for us to go on like this for days: he, issuing bright little optimistic statements, while my hys-teria and the little problem in the children's bathroom both rise to new levels.

Finally, of course, something has to be done. Getting a wrench is out of the question because our neighbor doesn't have one; we lost it for him the last time we borrowed it. So instead of a wrench, we get the next best thing: a brother-in-law.

A brother-in-law is someone married to your sister who has a wrench and is a whiz with plumbing. And if you want to get philosophical about it, because he is a relative, he has a certain moral obligation to involve himself in any emergency you might have.

I'm so frantic by this time I'm ready to involve any-body. But my brother-in-law is a nice guy. He's a fast worker too. He had every pipe dismantled before you could say never mind. It only took him two hours to find out there was a lot more wrong with those bathroom pipes than we had guessed.

In fact, it was so bad we were going to need a plumber. And quick. But my brother-in-law's trip wasn't a total loss. He forgot his wrench.

No Speaka Da Real Estate 🐝 Because

we are selling one house and looking for another, we have discovered a whole new vocabulary. You might even say a whole new language.

The natives who speak this language are found largely

in real estate offices and open houses. They are distinguished by their enthusiasm for dwellings of any sort. Their speech habits differ from ours in that they do not use such words as small, inadequate or old. Anything under 800 square feet is cozy; if there are two bedrooms and you wanted three, it has build-on possibilities; and houses built in 1904 aren't old–they're older.

The natives never say service porch–it's the laundry area; and that table in the hall with the phone on it is the planning center.

Your house isn't clean, it's immaculate. If it's next to a supermarket and across from a drive-in movie, it's near everything. And if it has been condemned it's a fixer-upper.

This show of linguistic optimism is contagious, and you may find yourself using it at the drop of a listing.

"Don't put that clay on the high-quality wool carpeting, Freddie, or I'll have to lock you in your play area."

The natives may drop in for impromptu runs through the house with a buyer at any hour. This is all to the good, of course, as any one of these visits may put an end to any future calls.

But there is still the problem of what to do with yourself. At the onset you were warned not to skulk along the hallway after buyers, eavesdropping for favorable comments.

"Get lost," you were told; only the natives say it, "Let us stay with the buyer."

So when you see them coming, you run out to the garage and busy yourself in a far corner with a box of Snarol. It's better that way anyway–makes the house look bigger . . .

Can You Hear Me, Tom Edison? 🐝 I can't be sure, of course, but

I'm beginning to suspect that the reason Thomas Edison took so many of those catnaps he was famous for was that he was born in the same year as Alexander Graham Bell. That's right, 1847.

While prolific Thomas was working on such quiet inventions as the light bulb and the camera, that rascal Alexander was down in his basement perfecting the telephone.

I further suspect that just as tired Thomas laid his weary bones down for what he hoped would be a good eight hours of sleep, Alexander phoned him.

"Hello! Hello! Can you hear me, Tom?" Alexander must have said, because two such brilliant contemporaries must have known each other.

"Yes, yes," tired Thomas answered, "I can hear you. Now hang up so I can get some sleep."

Alexander, hurt, replied, "I'm sorry I woke you."

And Thomas, kind as well as gifted, answered, "Oh, I was just taking a little catnap. It's all right."

Then, as soon as Alexander would begin to doubt that he had really done it, really put a human voice on wire, he'd call Edison again just to make sure. So that finally, every time poor Thomas Edison tried to get a little sleep, the phone would ring.

The whole process was repeated so many times that Alexander came to believe that Thomas was a fool for work and slept only in bits and pieces. No matter how Edison tried to change his sleeping hours, Alexander Graham Bell always interrupted them.

"Another catnap?" Alexander would say. "Man, don't you ever get a good, straight eight hours?"

And apparently he never picked up the note of frustration in Edison's voice when he'd answer, "Almost never."

And so it was, I believe, that Thomas Edison's sleeping habits came to be misunderstood by so many. For as soon as Alexander Graham Bell had all the bugs out of his telephone, at the young age of only twenty-nine, he called everybody he knew and told them how Tom Edison never really got any decent shuteye.

Bartlett's Quotations doesn't list it, of course, but I believe it was Thomas Edison who first said, "Never trust anybody under thirty."

Mama Mia, Round Spaghetti 🥄 There is a canned spaghetti on the market that is as insidious a product as I have seen in a long time. The pitch is that it is shaped like an O and can be eaten with a spoon.

Now I ask you, what kind of challenge is that for our children? No more struggles of any kind, kiddies, Daddy will drive you the two blocks to the baseball field where you will be allowed your turn at bat or mommy will speak to the coach.

And when you come home, junior dear, you can have a nice big bowl of round spaghetti that won't slip off your spoon.

Next it may be hybrid apples without cores so kids won't have to walk to trash cans.

Or drinking straws with pumps so our darlings won't have to exert themselves sucking.

But if we take a stand right now on round spaghetti, it may not be too late.

Snap off that TV commercial which promises kids a cheap victory and make a big caldron of the longest, slipperiest spaghetti you can find.

Cover it with a sauce that is both succulent and slimy.

Hand the child a fork and let him cope. If he's been on round spaghetti too long, he may have withdrawal symptoms and whine for a spoon. But stand firm, old dear, stand firm.

And remember, as he struggles with the strands, that there is nothing like a plate of good old-fashioned spaghetti to fulfill a child.

To fulfill him and help him to realize, on his own, that round spaghetti is really very square.

Sick of the Hospital 🐛 A hospital is a

place where the cheapest room is $154 a day and they don't even have a tennis court. It's a place where as soon as you're able to eat the food it's time to go home. It's where beautiful nurses always say yes to a man—when he asks if he absolutely must have that shot.

When my husband found these things out recently he called me to his bedside and said: "Get me out of here." Fortunately his illness was not serious, but while tests were being done, he was being undone.

"Relax," I told him. "Look at the nice view you have of the parking lot."

He refused to look. I asked him if he'd like me to bring him a rose and a box of English tea cookies.

"Hell, no," he said. "Bring me my old Boy Scout handbook so I can look up knot tying. I've got two sheets here, and there's a linen supply closet across the hall where I can get more. I think I could make it out the window and down the side of the building."

I patted his hand and asked, "In that gown?"

He scowled. "Bring me that handbook and my pants."

When I told him it might be two days before the hospital would release him, he rang for the nurse and reminded her that kidnapping was a serious offense. She only smiled and took his temperature.

And when he finally did go home, down that sterile hall, sitting in a wheelchair, holding enough flowers to qualify him as a float in the Rose Parade, he looked a little sheepish.

"Thanks," he said to a bevy of nurses who had gathered to bid him good-bye. "You are all part angel." He meant it, too.

Better Secretive Than Sorry 🐝 The

other day a friend who is a consummate cook served me a piece of lemon pie with an apology. "I'm sorry about the filling," she said, "but it stuck to the pan and lumped a little."

Before she mentioned it, I had been impressed with the filling's texture and assumed it was another of her culinary triumphs. The incident reminded me of my husband's grandmother's cream-filled doughnuts.

This wonderful old lady had a large family and loved to cook. She had prepared more meals than Howard Johnson. For the first two weeks of our marriage my time was largely devoted to trying, without success, to duplicate her doughnuts. Try putting a cream filling in a doughnut sometime.

When I asked the grandmother her secret, she only changed the subject and gave me a Mona Lisa smile.

Finally, in a fit of frustration, I conceded and admitted that there are some things only a grandmother can give a man.

But hope springs eternal, and years later at a family reunion I drew one of the relatives aside and asked him if he knew where I might get the recipe for grandmother's marvelous cream-filled doughnuts.

"Cream-filled!" he hooted. "Why, the old lady made the worst doughnuts in town! They were her one failing: always half-done. That wasn't cream filling; it was batter!"

And the funny thing is, even knowing, my husband still talks about those doughnuts. I'd know how to make then now, but somehow I don't think my half-done doughnuts could ever compare to his grandmother's half-done doughnuts. For what can extinguish the eternal flame of boyhood memories?

So the next time your pie is lumpy or your doughnuts half-done, serve them with great aplomb. Who knows, you may be starting a legend.

New Year Revolutions 🕊 Some people

break their clavicles; I break my resolutions. But this year it's going to be different, because, like broken clavicles, broken resolutions come from taking risks.

You're not going to hear me promise never to eat chocolate-covered cherries again. Hell, no. I'm just going to promise never to eat them on the Tuesdays I see a giant condor sitting on my front porch.

Same thing with my talking. I'm not going to say I'll stop, because I do it all the time. But from now on I resolve to be quiet the minute the person I'm talking to falls asleep. And I'll never interrupt again unless I'm going to say something.

Reform is easy with realistic goals. Take my hall closet. It's a mess. But I'm not going in there with leather gloves and a pitchfork. I'm not going to rummage among all those boxes on the top shelf where I might find snapshots from 1952.

The last time I did that I didn't come out of the closet for two days. I'll simply raise my right hand and cross my heart never to open the door unless the cat gets trapped in there. Maybe not even then–what a way to keep cat hairs off the sofa.

I'm looking forward to 1981 not because there's going to be a new me, but because there's going to be a true me. I'm going to stop trying to be that woman in the ads who lays a family room floor of self-sticking squares and looks cheerful.

When I lay those squares I'm going to frown and moan and make a big deal out of it.

I'm going to be just a plain, ordinary housewife with limits, a woman who will work only twelve hours a day and then sit down–whether she's tired or not. A woman who knows how to say no to her children.

"No," I'll say to my kids, "I will not drive you downtown right now. You can walk. You can walk over to the table and get my car keys."

All it takes is a little determination and you can do it, too.

Close as Pages in a Book 🐞 I keep

hearing about the "generation gap," but we don't have any such thing at our house. It may be our floor plan, or maybe the acoustics, but it is darn near impossible to put any kind of distance between me and my kids.

I mean, they keep reaching me. I needed a gap in the worst way last Saturday when my son came home from the school puppet show.

"I'm gonna tell you all about it," he said. And he did. Only his version took two hours and the show had lasted only 40 minutes.

"Are you listening?" he demanded, when my eyes began to wander after the first hour.

"Oh, I am, I am," I assured him, but, quite frankly, I think Albee has more punch than Judy.

And there's no gap at all between my daughter and me when it comes to dresses–we wear the same size. She has no trouble communicating how she feels about it, either.

"Oh, mother," she wailed when I showed her my new dress, "it just isn't me."

"You bet your sweet boots it isn't," I said. "This dress is not supposed to be you. It's designed for me–a woman who wants to look with-it, but is really running along behind it."

She looked petulant, and for a minute I thought she was going to get mad and go to her room. No luck. She followed me into my bedroom and headed for my dressing table–another "no gap" area.

"Can I borrow your eye shadow?" she asked.

"Not until you return my eyebrow pencil, my eyelash curler and my hair spray."

"Jeez!" she said, and flounced out.

But not for long. She was back in five minutes with the announcement that it was my turn to drive her friends to the "away" game and I only had a half hour to pick up seven girls and drive them ten miles.

As I say, we have no gap at our house. Our communication is close, constant and wild. But to tell you the truth, I'd give anything for a good old-fashioned afternoon gap.

Keep a Light Burning over the Sink for Me 🦋 Men, don't worry about

how your wife will manage the money if you should never return some night.

Financially she is way ahead of you, but for heaven's sake, tell her now–before it's too late–how to replace the light bulb over the sink.

And if you don't see why it should be so difficult, try secreting yourself in the broom closet sometime and watch her have a go at it. It is not a pretty sight.

Only last week, after begging my husband to replace the burned-out light over our sink, I had to face the job alone and unaided.

He had left for a weekend business trip, and how could a man who forgets his razor be expected to think about light bulbs?

He can't, he doesn't, and he didn't.

So, realizing full well that most fatal accidents happen in the home, I dragged a kitchen chair over to the edge of the sink. Funny, I never noticed until that moment that the light over our sink is recessed.

For those of you not in the construction business, that means it's flush with the ceiling.

Looks great, but how do you get into it? Well, first you have to get up there.

So you put one foot on the sink and one foot on the water faucet, boost, and then grab either side of the recessed light. This turns all ten of your fingernails backward until they touch your first knuckle.

But you have hold of it, and even though the blood is rushing to your elbows, you don't give up.

With tattered fingertips, you work it gently back and forth, but it won't budge until your foot slips off the faucet and plunges into the garbage disposer.

That's just the force you needed, and the whole fixture comes off–along with a fine shower of five dead moths, six petrified flies, and something with long, thin legs that is still moving.

Then you remember you left the light bulb in the other room. So you go get it–after you take your foot out of the garbage disposer. You were going to anyway, because the seven-year-old turned it on. Open-toed shoes are back, but you'll never be able to wear them now. The light over the sink does go on, however, and not since those nurses decided to stay on Corregidor has any woman been braver.

What's Brewing at Home? 🐝 In

swinging London, tavern keepers report an income drop of 60 percent. It's a rather sobering percentage if you happen to run an English tavern. It's enough to drive a bloke to drinking his own stuff.

This is exactly what the poor fellows might have to do if the present do-it-yourself beer and wine kits keep selling like they are. A recent law providing drastic penalties for car drivers who drink more than they should and then drive has prompted beer and wine making in the cozy atmosphere of the suburban family kitchen.

The British are using plastic garbage cans to whip up their joy juice, and retailers report that sales of these have trebled. Well, home-brewing may have solved the problem of driving, but I should think there would be other drawbacks.

I mean, say you are sitting around some Friday evening and suddenly your husband decides he wants a beer. "Any beer in the garbage can, honey?" he asks brightly.

"No, dear," you answer. "Would you like me to make some?"

If there is anything a man likes to see, it is his wife bustling around the kitchen, so of course he tells you to go ahead. You get out the plastic garbage can, along with 4 pounds of hops, 12 cups of malt, and 35 gallons of whatever else it takes.

You are stirring this concoction with the broom handle when your seven-year-old walks in with a group of neighborhood children.

Now, it is one thing to have a six-pack in the refrigerator, but quite another to be busy at the still whipping up 50 gallons. Quickly you slap the lid on the garbage can and smile innocently at the children.

One of the more precocious boys with eyes like Al Capone's sniffs the air knowingly and asks, "Makin' beer?"

You are at a loss for words.

But your seven-year-old isn't. "So what if she is!" he snaps defensively. "Your mother stomps grapes."

"No she never!" shrieks the Capone type. This sort of argument isn't covered in the childcare books, but I think it would be safe to say it is important for mother to keep her head–which is probably more than she can say for her beer.

Singing Auld Lang Syne in a Very Low Key 🐞 There was a song, back

in the forties, that used to ask, "What are you doing New Year's . . . New Year's Eve?"

And, in those days, what I did on New Year's Eve was of paramount importance to me. But as the years roll by I find I am inclined to answer such an inquiry with a Gallic shrug. I really don't know what I'll be doing, to tell you the truth, but I do know what I won't be doing.

I will not be at a big party in silver shoes that hurt my feet.

I will not be assuring someone else's husband that he is too a good dancer as he kicks my toe three inches back into my shoe.

I will not be at a cocktail party, talking in earnest to a woman I only just met, about her child's sinus condition.

I will not be in a nightclub eating a $50 dinner which I could duplicate at home for $5. I don't care if they do give me a paper hat and a horn to blow.

I won't be down the street at the neighborhood bash either. It may be a little embarrassing to say no, but not half as embarrassing as facing them all the next morning.

And count me out when it comes to joining another couple for a weekend celebration in some secluded mountain cabin. What a setup for one of our seven collective children, left at home, to come down with something. I can see the ranger now, knocking on the cabin door and telling us to knock off all the revelry–there is a postnasal infection at home.

No, I can't really tell you what I'll be doing. But I can tell you this much: I am seriously toying with the idea of staying home. It's in my price range, and I won't have to worry about what to wear.

The kids will be asleep by midnight, leaving my husband and me alone in the living room with our bottle of domestic champagne. And domestic champagne is the best kind for the sort of celebration I have in mind.

Ecology Begins at Home 🐝 I won't say

my children are ecology nuts, because I think anybody who isn't ecology-minded has to be a bit loony. But I will say my kids have an enthusiasm about it that can be unnerving.

"Mom," my boy exclaimed last week, "you don't have a brick in your toilet!"

"Well, I should hope not!" I said. "I know I'm not the best housekeeper in the world, and I may have small living creatures in my flour bin, but there hasn't been a woman in our family for generations with a brick in her toilet."

"That's just the point," answered my twelve-year-old. "You should have a brick in your toilet tank to replace water volume for conservation."

He was right, of course, so what do you say to a kid like that except go get me a brick?

It was the same thing when I bought colored tissue for the bathroom. After fifteen years, finally everything in that room matched. Besides, I figured everybody would find it aesthetically rewarding to blow their noses on hot pink instead of plain old white.

But not my daughter. As soon as she discovered the colored tissue, she ran toward me brandishing a handful of it and said, "Mother! You're killing the fish!"

"What fish?" I answered. "Your goldfish passed on to his reward two years ago."

"No, no," she said impatiently, "the ones in the ocean! The dye in colored tissue isn't good for them."

So now I have to forgo all those exotic colors and keep telling myself: if it's white, it's right.

But I'll tell you what really has me worried. Recently a bill requiring courts to reward persons who give information leading to the conviction of litterbugs was passed by the Assembly in Sacramento and sent to the Senate.

And my kids have been watching me. I think they remember that two weeks ago I threw a gum wrapper out of a moving car. I don't know what came over me, and I'm sorry; I really am.

But my kids won't listen to excuses like that. So tonight, after they're asleep, I'm going out with a flashlight and look for the wrapper. I threw it out somewhere between Elm Avenue and John Street.

If I'm quick about it, they may not turn me in.

The Voice of the Teacher 🍎 It's parent-teacher conference time again.

For mothers of children in the upper grades, this is a fairly routine review of achievement-behavior patterns, and after at least seven previous sessions, mother knows pretty well what to expect in revelations from the teacher.

But in the lower grades, especially kindergarten and first grade, mother enters that conference room with the same high expectations she had in the delivery room.

It is the teacher's task to raise the shade on truth without letting reality hurt mother's eyes.

And teachers, being teachers, ease the discomfort with the use of vocabulary.

When Miss White tells mother her son has a high activity level and shows an aggressive attitude, it is better than hearing that he won't sit still a minute and has hit another kid across the temple with a building block.

There is hope for future improvement when the teacher confides that he isn't doing work up to his capacity.

If little Freddie shows good reading readiness, that isn't as bad as saying he can't read yet.

If he needs structured play, isn't that nicer than saying he's a troublemaker at recess?

It is the final act of mercy when Miss White tells mom that Freddie has leadership qualities and is well liked by the other children in class.

What the good teacher really means is that all the others kids are pretty bad, but since Freddie is by far the worst, he leads all the others.

Head of the first-grade syndicate. Together, these thirty-one hardened six-year-olds will somehow reach the end of the school year–able to read, to do new math, and to stay clear of the law.

And the teacher, bless her, will take on a fresh batch of problems . . . or should I say a new group of students, in the vernacular of the parent-teacher conference?

Summer Visitation 🐝 Unless you happen to

live in Death Valley, a summer means houseguests.

And even in Death Valley there are probably a few dusty relatives looking for other relatives to drop in one day.

No matter how fond you may be of Cousin Fred, his wife Zelda and their three kids, the very thought of all five of them joining all five of you for even two or three days is unnerving.

Their postcard said: "Arrive noon Saturday. Don't go to any trouble. Bobby, Kevin and Jimmy can all sleep together."

If it were only a question of Bobby, Kevin and Jimmy sleeping, you wouldn't give it another thought; but the last time those kids came, they never hit the sack before 10:30.

You wonder what they mean by "Don't go to any trouble."

Getting the extra table leaf out from the back of the hall closet not only is trouble; it's downright dangerous.

Move that leaf, and the vacuum, the card table, two tennis racquets and a 500-piece bingo set crash onto your ankles.

Even if you manage to elongate the table, there's still the problem of what to put on it.

Cousin Zelda's appetite is merely gigantic, but Cousin Fred's is organic. He's a health food addict who smugly munches mysterious supplements to each meal. His general attitude about what you eat is that it's your funeral. You can't give a man like that white bread, and if you know what's good for you, you'll eat the crusts, too.

And the three boys hit the kitchen like a swarm of locusts, eating up one cupboard and down the other. The last time they left, there wasn't anything on the shelf but a box of dog biscuits and a can of lard.

190

All ten of you taking turns in the bathroom can be so time-consuming that Disneyland, Knott's Berry Farm and the Pacific Ocean remain unexplored.

They came 700 hundred miles to mill around in your hall waiting to get into the bathroom.

Since your health insurance doesn't cover nervous breakdown, their departure for home comes in the nick of time.

Smiling weakly, you wave farewell and promise to drop in on them sometime. It will serve them right if you do.

Post Office Blues:
Shake, Rattle, and Roll 🦋 Every time I

succeed in mailing a package, I feel as if I should write the Post Office Department a thank-you note.

There's a man at the package window who, I am sure, thinks I am out to blow up the place. I handed him a small brown parcel tied carefully with blue string and stood there, waiting.

He turned it over gingerly two or three times and then looked at me suspiciously.

"What's in this?" he asked through compressed lips.

"It's a cartridge," I answered innocently.

"Cartridge!" he boomed. "You don't mean a projectile for a firearm?"

The three people in the line behind me moved back, and a toddler in a stroller began to whimper.

"No, no," I said. "It's only film."

"Film?" he said, raising his eyebrows and giving me an I'm-onto-you-now look. Clearly, he thought I was a 007 type sending microfilm to a sinister character who would in turn pass it on to "Mr. Big."

I can't be sure, but I think he pressed a button on the floor with his foot, because another postal clerk appeared. Together they fondled the package, and then the second clerk regarded me gravely and said, "Lady, this rattles."

By now a crowd was forming and the whole thing was getting out of hand. Apparently, packages that rattle are just as suspect as packages that tick.

"I think I would rather have a dozen 15-cent stamps," I lied. "I don't really want to mail that package right now anyway."

They exchanged J. Edgar Hoover glances and gave the parcel back. The spectators made a path for me as I left the post office and I couldn't help but notice all those WANTED posters tacked to the walls. Poor devils, I thought, probably tried to mail packages that rattled. Or maybe they even licked an envelope with only a ten-cent stamp on it.

It started me thinking, and I went right home and memorized my ZIP Code. And I'm going to use it, too—one can't be too careful these days.

The Cat Is Fit 🐾 The next time you drop your cat into the washing machine for the full cycle, don't be too sure he's all washed up.

Take the case of Dinky, the cat from Eastleigh, England—better known to the boys on the back fence as "Dizzy Dink."

It seems old Dinky's mistress inadvertently tossed him in with the morning's wash one day. Poor woman had no idea Dinky was sleeping one off in the clothes hamper, so she didn't notice as she loaded her washer that her wash was loaded.

Imagine her surprise when she opened the door—after a 15-minute swirl-dry cycle—and out stepped Dinky, none the worse for wash-and-wear. Alarmed, Dinky's anxious owner hustled him off to the nearest veterinarian for a complete physical.

But she needn't have bothered. The vet allowed that although Dink had spun around with the wash approximately 800 times, he would survive.

You bet your puss and boots he would survive. I can see him now, flattened against the inside of the washer, calmly licking a forepaw as his master's socks flew past him for the 743rd time.

"This, too, will end," he no doubt thought, and of course he was right–as cats always are in their maddening way.

I used to think the nine-lives theory was a myth, but Dinky and his kind have convinced me it is a fact. Cats have an equanimity in the face of seeming disaster which we would all do well to emulate.

I've known women who were ready to give up on Monday morning–throw in the towel, so to speak–just contemplating the wash. But Dinky got right in with it and landed on his feet.

One cool cat. A little dizzy, maybe, but cool nevertheless.

Vacation Maladies 🐾 Now that summer is

on its way, it will soon be time for the family vacation. Basic health precautions are necessary to assure a good time by all.

There are four major vacation maladies to guard against.

First is backseat tension. When driving anywhere over 25 miles with more than one child, you are sure to develop this condition. It begins with name-calling and progresses into pinching and punching.

Since the kids cannot be sent to their rooms and they will not fit into the glove compartment, the backseat becomes a fight arena and mother and dad become victims of backseat tension.

Then there is souvenir disease. Everybody comes down with this one. Get more than five miles from home and suddenly you want to take whatever you find back with you. If you are lucky on a vacation, what you find is peace, insight and joy—which can never be brought home in a jar.

So don't bother with the matchbooks, ashtrays and other mementos. They will take up valuable room the kids need for their souvenirs, which will all be very large, very ugly and very useless.

Elevatoritis is a minor but annoying vacation illness usually contracted by boys under ten. You have to stay in a large hotel to get this one.

At first it seems a blessing that your boy is spending all his time in the elevator, but the looks you get from the other guests soon change all that.

Since there is little hope of getting the boy out of the elevator and you find it increasingly hard to face people, the remedy lies in using the stairways or, if you prefer, the fire escapes.

The final ailment is the most devastating and is known as hotel hysteria. It hits when you reach your destination and find, to your horror, that the spacious family room the hotel brochure pictured is actually a 15x10-foot cubicle with wall-to-wall beds.

The window faces another window which allows you to look directly into the eyes of a traveling salesman.

The bathroom can only be reached by snaking your way between suitcases, rollaway beds and all those souvenirs. Try it in the middle of the night and you'll go down to breakfast in a wheelchair.

So beware when you start out on that little family jaunt.

You may need more protection than a first aid kit can afford.

Letting a Sleeping Dog Lie 🐝 Charlie,

a giant poodle, went outside without his glasses and was lost for three weeks.

Shaggy dog story? Not at all. It really happened in Berkeley, California.

Charlie's specs are held in place by a strap around his head. I showed my dog the story in the newspaper, but he wasn't interested. "Why don't you ever go outside and participate in what's happening?" I asked Higgins, but he only rolled over on his back and sighed.

That's his trouble. No nose for news. All he ever wants to do is sleep and try new dog foods. He's so lazy he won't chase a car unless it's parked.

I took him to obedience school to learn how to wake up, but when they said "stay" he thought they said "lay," and by the time he woke up, the lesson was over. And he refused to go back.

Now don't tell me I'm bigger than the dog and I should have forced him. Did you ever try to get a dog who is practicing passive resistance into the backseat of a car? I got him as far as the front door and he went limp.

"Come on, Higgins," I said. "Want to have one of those new dog biscuits Art Linkletter showed you on TV?"

He opened one eye, saw I had my car keys in my hand, and closed it again. I suppose I could have dragged him down the driveway, but sometimes neighbors don't understand those things.

So I let him stay home.

It was weak, I know, but when that dog looks at me with those big, closed eyes, there isn't much I can do. I mean, who wants to argue with a dead dog? That's his one and only trick, and he's always "on."

And I'm convinced it's a trick, because all I have to do is open the refrigerator door and he comes to. Not for long, but he does get up on all fours and come toward me.

If I could just get him to go outside, I know he could make the headlines too. After all, a dog in glasses isn't so much. But a dog who walks all over town in his sleep–that's something!

A Boy with Tomorrow in His Eyes

🐝 For mothers of little boys, I would like to issue a warning: watch out for thirteen.

When my daughter turned thirteen, I wrote what I thought was a rather tender good-bye to her little-girl-hood. A girl at thirteen, whether she is yours or every woman's child, is as delightful as spring's first daffodil. There's an unfolding, a latent womanhood that has been there all along, and you know she has the situation well in hand.

But a boy at thirteen is as delightful as a 3-megaton bomb hidden in your basement with the fuse burning. I don't care how cute he was at two and a half, how dimpled his hands, how silken his hair–take a good look; you'll need it to fortify you later on.

Because, mom, a thirteen-year-old boy is not suddenly a man as a girl is a woman, he is only on his way. And what a way to go. To travel that path, nature equips him overnight with feet the size of his father's. Feet he insists on encasing in $20 athletic shoes which, he imagines, will help him run faster than Kip Keino, jump higher than Bob

Seagren, and make more baskets than Wilt Chamberlain.

These shoes are rarely off his feet, but when they are, all you have to do to find them is follow your nose. His socks are never clean, even directly from the washer, detergent commercials be damned. Thirteen's socks always look as if he had just finished a stroll over hot tar.

He eats only one meal a day: it lasts from sonup to sondown. There is nothing he won't swallow except advice. What he ever knew of table manners is abandoned, because his hands, once so cherublike, match his feet. Only his feet are cleaner.

He is like looking at the excavation site for a 50-story skyscraper: you know there's going to be something magnificent there someday, but it is a little hard to imagine. Except, maybe, when he looks up suddenly from his homework and forgets the now and has the future in his eyes. Then, he might say something surprisingly wise and fine. And you know. Thirteen is rough, no doubt about it; but tomorrow's on its way.

The Rising Cost of
Cheap Thrills ✺ New York's Coney Island has
done away with its penny arcade. Now it's the quarter arcade.

This only goes to prove it is a lot more expensive to keep a kid amused today.

I can remember going into a penny arcade at age nine with 83 cents and my lunch. When I staggered out at dusk, fingers numb from pulling levers back, I had not only six cents change, but the sweet sensation of having turned my back on everything a penny could buy.

Now, a kid will have to be self-supporting to spend much time in the quarter arcade. Coney Island will become a hangout for children of the rich. "Dad," a boy of ten will say, "give me \$15 to go to the quarter arcade."

Father will answer, "You've been there three times this week. You'll have to make a choice–either you cut out the rifle range, fortune-teller machine and the prize crane–or give up Yale. I can't manage both."

Poor little rich kid. Just another victim of today's rising costs–pitching quarters instead of pennies. And, I suppose, along with raising the price level, the arcade people will also raise the prize level.

When a kid can afford to sink \$15 into the bowling game and manual crane, he isn't likely to want the sort of reward I carried home in 1932–a two-inch bulldog with a pipe in his mouth and a Speak-No-Evil monkey with a chipped ear.

Today's kid will want a waterproof calendar watch and a transistor radio. Of course he already has a watch and a radio of his own at home, but then I had another bulldog with a pipe, too.

So maybe it is just a matter of changing times, and my children's children will be going to the dollar arcade to try for a minibike.

In the meantime, however, if I thought the quarter arcade had raised the prize level, and I could work that crane around just right to pick up a transistor radio, well, why not? After all, I've had my fill of bulldogs.

The Carpenter
Is Always Right 🍎 We are having a little

remodeling done at our house and, like having a baby, you forget what it's like until you go through it again.

I had forgotten what the personality of a carpenter is like.

I know that's a generalization, but–really–they all do the same things. Right in the middle of telling them what you want done to the wardrobe closet doors, they will unfailingly start to chuckle softly and begin to shake their heads.

"What's so funny?" I asked my latest hammer-and-saw man. "I mean, if there's a joke or something, let me in on it."

"Lady," he said, "you gals are all alike. You aren't gonna like those doors when you get 'em. They open too wide."

He liked the ones already on the closet, which were so heavy I had to wear a truss when I pushed them open.

I told him I wanted wideopen doors so I could see at a glance what I didn't have to wear.

"Well, OK," he finally said, "but you aren't gonna like 'em."

And just to show what the power of negative nailing can do–sure enough, I didn't like 'em. But not because they opened too wide. I didn't like those doors because he put the knobs that opened them up so high I had to get on a stool to reach them.

When I mentioned this to him, he looked surprised and said, "Why didn't you say something sooner?" I can't believe he didn't see me out there in the garage an hour before–motioning to him through a blizzard of sawdust and shouting over the whine of his power saw, "Sam, you made the knobs too high."

I said it as soon as I noticed it, but carpenters like you to say it before they do it. And how can you, when they won't tell you what they are going to do next?

Whenever you ask, they start that clucking and headshaking again and say, "You gals are all alike."

But I think I have the knob problem solved. I'll just have him build me a couple of stairs in front of the closet–only then the doors won't open, will they?

At least not so wide, which is, after all, the way he wanted it in the first place.

Kids Show
Dogs and Confidence 🦋 Last Saturday

morning a dog food company threw an amateur dog show just for kids in the parking lot of our local supermarket. My son entered his dog, a 200-pound Newfoundland, and I went along to watch the fur fly.

"Every kid in town with a dog will be there," I told him, "so hold onto that beast, or we'll be sued for terrorizing the parking lot."

"Mom," my son answered patiently, "Noche graduated fourth in his class from obedience school. He will stay when I tell him to."

So I dropped them off and stayed myself to watch. Dogs of mixed heritage and dogs of recognizable breeds were leashed and waiting to be judged in their class.

My son led Noche over to compete for the title of "Largest Dog," and he won paws down. An Irish setter gave him a dirty dog look, and Noche gave him one back which said clearly, "That's the luck of the Irish, setter."

But the setter entered the "Best Trick" class next, and our dog could only stand and drool. My son patted him and said "Lay," and Noche collapsed in a heap to watch the other dogs excel.

One little girl in line knelt beside a brown mutt and whispered, "You're next, so try hard." Her dog was the size of a small coyote and his head looked like a transplant. He had fine eyes, but one ear was pointing north and the other south.

When at last their turn came they marched smartly into center ring while the competition looked on. The mutt stood facing the little girl as she said, "Sit up." He wagged his tail.

She said "Roll over," and he sat down. "Speak," she implored, and he bounded over and licked her hand. "Don't worry," she said as they left the ring, "you still might win 'Best of Show.' "

That's what I call confidence. And confidence is what it's all about, because half the dogs there had no papers, except the ones on the kitchen floor, and most of them had more fleas than blue ribbons.

But they were all winners that Saturday morning in the parking lot, because they all had the love of a kid on the end of their leash.

Hold That Cafeteria Line ❦ A cafeteria's appeal is based on speed and economy. At noon one can slip in, run down the counter with a tray, and select, from any number of delectable dishes, something to hold body and soul together until dinner. Or so I thought.

Recently, after I had taken the children to the dentist and discovered they had no cavities, we decided to celebrate and popped gaily into a local cafeteria for what I thought would be a nice cheap lunch.

"Here, kids," I said, handing them both a tray, "pick up something that looks good to you, but steer clear of that roast tom turkey with country gravy and grandmother's stuffing, because that's $3, and we want to keep the price down this trip."

The seven-year-old wanted a hamburger, which is the one thing they don't have in a cafeteria, but the twelve-year-old knew exactly what she wanted. Everything.

She steered clear of the roast tom turkey, but she did a U-turn around everything else. She put so many plates on her tray that she looked like a busboy. It took two of us to get it to the table. I left her salting it all and went to look for the seven-year-old, whom I found amongst the desserts, happily loading them onto his tray with all the abandon of Diamond Jim Brady.

"Look here," I said, with as much authority as I could muster, "all those sweets will give you diabetes." The man behind him, who probably had no children, gave me a Mayo Brothers look. The woman who was dispensing the desserts gave me a "when did this kid eat last" look.

So I let him keep the apple pie, chocolate cake and cherries flambeau. But I made him put back the rice pudding. I'm nobody's fool.

I'll have to admit it was a pretty good lunch, considering the fact I didn't have a tray. I ate everything they left.

However, for the money, we could have gone to Chasen's and seen Cary Grant with our chocolate cake.

Come to think of it, the cavities would have been cheaper.

Profile in Cowardice ❦ All of us are called

upon, at one time or another, to use our courage.

Marie Antoinette used it on her way to the guillotine; I use it on my way to the dentist.

I realize there's really no comparison, because Marie's ordeal ended as soon as the drums stopped rolling and the blade dropped.

Five minutes at the most.

In my case, the need to exert courage may last as long as an hour and a half.

Only by facing reality in its starkest form, only by realizing that I'm going to have to go into that office and see it through, only then do I find the courage to stand up on my hind legs and faint.

In the reception room, all is serene.

"Flower Drum Song" escapes from an unseen slot in the wall. As I sat there shredding a magazine, it occurs to me that if I am as close as I'll ever be to my present dental appointment, I am, at the same time, as far as I'll ever be from my next dental appointment.

This desperate bit of rationalization gives me the strength to rise and stumble after the nurse when she beckons me to the chair.

The dentist enters.

There is a trend today for men of medicine to wear colored smocks. This is designed to fool the patient into thinking they are barbers.

At the same time, there is a trend for barbers to wear medical coats designed to fool the public into thinking they are doctors.

At any rate, it isn't the sort of masquerade than can be carried on successfully for long.

When he flicks on the light under your X-rays and you see your own teeth smiling back at you in all their grotesque glory, there can be no doubt: he is a dentist.

But if your dentist is perceptive, as mine is, he will ease the tension by giving you little things to do to make you feel useful and needed.

Things like keeping your tongue out of the way of a 250,000 rpm drill and paying your bill at the end of the month.

And who knows, by the time you pay the bill, you may be so preoccupied with building up your bank account that you will have forgotten all about building up your courage.

Housekeeping This Side
of the Law 🐝 An old man of 102 made news

recently when his neighbors had him jailed for refusing to

clean up his house. "When you get to be my age," he declared, "it doesn't matter if your house is clean or not."

Many a woman who feels 102 will be inclined to agree with this gentleman's philosophy. She might agree with him, but she would never come right out and say so. That's why I can't help feeling he is languishing in jail today—not because of his slovenly housekeeping, but because, even after 102 years of practice, he can't keep house like a woman. He's not cunning enough.

If some kindly woman had taken him in hand and shown him how to shake a dust mop out the front door at 8 A.M. to create the impression of early-bird industry, it might have helped him. If he had known how to run a dry cloth over his front windows once a week in plain view of the neighbors, they might never have guessed.

One of the girls should have tipped him off about hiding the matches after cleaning the ashtrays. Or told him to join a coffee club so he could have announced, "I'm going home and really clean that house of mine from top to bottom."

If you say things like that often enough, people get the idea you're a good housekeeper. Above all, he should never have answered his doorbell. (As it turned out, they only came over to arrest him anyway.)

If he had plugged in the vacuum he could have pretended he didn't hear the bell; and the callers, hearing the roar, would have pictured him cleaning furiously on the other side of the door. In reality, he would have been stretched out on the sofa reading the racing form. Some men never learn. If women hadn't figured out how to beat the rap, a lot of us would be doing time right now . . .

Call Me Mother–
Three Hundred and Sixty-Five
Days a Year 🐝 On May 11, mothers every-
where will be honored on what the advertisers have come
to call "her day." And heaven help the poor child,
whatever his age, who doesn't have a gift, commensurate
with his affection for her, stashed away ready for mother
on "her day."

Sons, daughters and husbands have been reminded for
two weeks by full-page ads of all the things poor old
mother doesn't have.

Back in 1907, when the whole thing started, a cornuco-
pia made by tiny hands and filled with wildflowers
probably was the extent of the gift-giving. And nobody
felt guilty about it. But now, anybody who can read
knows love is for sale, and if you can't swing it this
month, put it on the installment plan–if you care at all.
Because, according to the copywriters, mother will hang
on as best she can until May 11 when you can give her all
those things to make her life complete.

Like a water-powered toothpick. Or an electric knife.

But the one I like is that big $80 upright vacuum
cleaner. Boy, is that going to give some mother a nice
warm feeling every time she plugs it in and goes after all
that nasty old dirt on the living room rug. She will choke
up every time she empties the bag.

If the ads don't get you, habit will. I know one mother
who has twelve bedjackets and never wears them. But her
kids keep giving them to her.

And how about the classics? A box of candy filled
caramels and Brazil nuts to a mother with dentures? Or a
book you've always wanted to read? You might even treat
mom to dinner out so you won't have to cook it.

If all this sounds as if I don't believe in Mother's Day,

it's because I don't. I don't believe in one day to honor mother, any more than I believe in being a good mother one day a year. They are both full-time devotions.

This Sunday I just want to wake up to a houseful of the usual morning sounds—happy kids squealing, doors slamming, dog barking, and milkman closing the back gate.

How lucky I am.

Who needs a water-powered toothpick?